MORE PRAISE FOR *THE GRACE IN AGING*

One of *Spirituality & Practice*'s Best Spiritual Books of 2014

A *Foreword Reviews* IndieFab Winner

"A bracing but gentle wake-up call for anyone who wishes to understand and come to terms with the aging process and the universal impermanence of life itself."—*Booklist*

"Readers of all ages can gain an awareness of the joy inherent in everyday moments large and small. Singh's calming and illuminating prose aims to bring a sense of liberation to readers' lives and open their minds to a world full of love, laughter, and peace."—*Shelf Awareness*

"*The Grace in Aging* establishes guideposts in the fog for those seeking greater meaning and fulfillment as they edge toward life's grand finale; Singh urges us to reclaim the process of aging. The impact is exhilaration."—*Spirituality and Health*

THE GRACE IN AGING

AWAKEN AS YOU GROW OLDER

Kathleen Dowling Singh

Wisdom Publications
199 Elm Street
Somerville, MA 02144 USA
wisdomexperience.org

Library of Congress Cataloging-in-Publication Data
Singh, Kathleen Dowling, author.
The grace in aging : awaken as you grow older / Kathleen Dowling Singh.
pages cm
Includes index.
ISBN 1-61429-126-8 (pbk. : alk. paper) — ISBN 978-1-61429-150-3 (eBook)
1. Aging—Religious aspects. 2. Aging—Psychological aspects. I. Title.
BL65.A46S56 2014
204′.40846—dc23
2014000597

ISBN 978-1-61429-126-8 ebook ISBN 978-1-61429-150-3

24 23
8 7 6

Cover design by Judith Arisman and Gopa&Ted2, Inc., inspired by a design by Bethany Singh. Interior design by Gopa&Ted2. Set in Palatino LT Std 10.5/15.8. Author photo by Barbara Banks.

Wisdom Publications' books are printed on acid-free paper and meet the guidelines for permanence and durability of the Production Guidelines for Book Longevity of the Council on Library Resources.

Printed in the United States of America.

Please visit fscus.org.

With healing the hallmark
of each and every step,
and grace the tender reward.

—Ken Wilber

CONTENTS

PREFACE

THE PROFOUND SPIRITUAL TEACHER Wei Wu Wei calls any conversation about awakening "the most important discussion to be had." This book is an offering to that conversation, "not because you do not know the truth . . . but because you know it already"(1 John 2:21).

My wish is that your reflection on the questions posed throughout this book will stir and deepen whatever longing you may ever have had to awaken, to reach the deep, still heart of the great mystery we call life. It can be illuminating to pause with each question and explore and contemplate our own unique answers. The "Questionnaire on Aging," the appendix, offers an additional opportunity for some deep reflection as to how you wish to spend the last years of your life.

I have tried to speak ecumenically, in broad strokes, to underscore the one Dharma, the one truth underlying all wisdom traditions. If you are far along a particular path, you will note where some words or sentences are not quite accurate or resonant within the view of your path. Translate. Use the words here lightly for inspiration and the words of your own tradition precisely for progress.

My endless gratitude goes to all of the kind teachers who guided me toward making my life such a rich one. In particular, Rodney Smith's penetrating insights have been enormous gifts.

My gratitude also goes to my children, grandchildren, and brothers for all of the support and love and joy that they have always given me. To my *sangha*, dear circle of spiritual friends, thank you for all you have meant for all of this time.

I also want to thank all of the aging and dying and grieving and growing people who have shared themselves with me and taught me so much.

To my generation, especially now as we enter our last chapters: may we all grow in the beauty, peace, and grace of awakening.

INTRODUCTION

The Grace in Aging approaches a topic that is, like death and dying, both difficult to contemplate and to experience. Aging and dying are topics that we tend to resist exploring in any but the most superficial of ways. We quite often hold them at arm's length or keep them hidden away or view them as somehow relating more to someone else's future. The truth, which many of us would prefer to resist, is that both aging, if we live long enough, and dying are inherent, inevitable aspects of every human life. The energy involved in resisting the truth of both aging and dying can keep us confined in a limited experience of living, a limited experience of the simple joy of being here now.

Dying is a naturally transformative experience in a human life. In the process of dying, we are freed from our confinement in the sense of self, the very source and site of our suffering and our separation from the sacred. In that freeing, awareness previously held in limitation, in self-reference, is released into awareness that is radiant and complete and holy. There is something undeniably powerful and sacred in either being a witness to another's dying or being the one in the process of coming close to death.

Although the dying process holds hope for deep, natural psychospiritual transformation, we cannot necessarily find hope in the process of aging in and of itself. It is certainly possible to experience aging with some real measures of denial or unmindfulness. There are many who enter the end of life, at ripe old ages, untapped and unexamined and filled with virtually as much confusion and unease as they were throughout all of the decades of their lives.

There seem to be a number of reasons why this is so. Aging moves more slowly than dying; it is a bit more muted in its urgency and a bit more imperceptible. It lacks the focus and sharp, compelling sequentiality of the process of active dying. Although it becomes a little bit harder to do so each day, aging still permits us to evade the truth of our own impermanence in a way that dying does not. Such evasions obstruct awakening.

Aging simply does not have the gathered intensity of dying. That gathered intensity, with all of the accompanying special conditions it engenders, is a crucible for transformation, for awakening. Simply aging, simply becoming an elderly person, offers no such transformative crucible. There is nothing in the process of simply getting older that, in and of itself, is going to make our eventual decline and illness and all of our losses either transformative or hopeful.

Whatever transformative experience we have of aging is dependent upon our own intention.

There are many ways to deal with living our older years. There are seventy-nine million of us in our generation just in the United States. Many ways to approach aging will be chosen, either deliberately or by default. Some ways will have more wisdom and will lead to more peace than others; some ways will lack wisdom and will lead to more stress and hopelessness and bewilderment, the phenomenon psychologist Erik Erikson called "ego despair."

The Grace in Aging speaks directly to those who have been stirred in their lifetime by the wish to awaken, to live in more sane, more kind, and more peaceful minds, to live in a more deeply sensed connection with the sacred. Hundreds of thousands of those of us who are aging have dabbled in awakening practices, flirted with them, perhaps even made such practices and the longing that drives the practices a real and present part of our lives.

This book is directed at all those who recognize that these older years are all that remain of our time to commit and devote to awakening. This time of our life can be seen to offer, to all of those who so choose, an opportunity to move our desire to awaken from a peripheral aspect of our lives to a central place—and on, even, to being the very reason for and experience of our moment-by-moment living.

The Grace in Aging comes from the perspective that with some outer vistas closing as we age, we would do well to recognize that inner vistas, peaceful and joyful and beautiful beyond imagining, can open. These inner vistas have always been within, available to us; we often just didn't have the time to explore them in any depth while we were immersed in the busy-ness of our lives to date.

Aging can offer us the time to deliberately reorient ourselves toward the inner life, an infinitely more reliable refuge than anything the world can offer. To open these inner vistas is to enter a time of awakening, to lighten our attachment to self, the cause of all of our unease. We have the opportunity to, first, recognize that living attached to our own sense of self is a small, confined, and stressed way to live and, then, to wholeheartedly engage in practices that will free that myopic attachment.

Lightening our attachment to self is the only thing that is going to get us through the decline, illness, and loss that we will, almost inevitably, face from now until we die with some equanimity and peaceful sanity, rather than with weeping and the gnashing of teeth.

Using these last years of our life as a time to awaken can help us cope and even grow in love and wisdom as we confront decline, illness, and loss. There are other benefits. We can give ourselves, finally, the experience of freedom and illumination and grace while still in the midst of life. We can, also, with our own spiritual ripening, offer all those younger ones who follow behind us in our spiritually impoverished culture the witness that awakening is possible.

Because the process of aging each day does not provide the circumstances that facilitate awakening, we ourselves need to create the causes and gather the conditions to do so. These causes and conditions are revealed in the dying process. There is much that the living can learn from the dying. These causes and conditions are skillful means, taught in all authentic spiritual traditions. Creating the causes and gathering the conditions of transformation in these later decades of our life will enable us to reveal and experience our own essential nature, to open into the grace of awakening far before we die.

We can, if we so choose, dedicate these last years to waking up.

Many of the words and thoughts in these pages offer an overview of spiritual practice that is appropriate for a person of any age. Viewed through the lens of aging, though, they take on a sense of both urgency and invitation. Each chapter is a contemplation, offering views to consider and steps to take—for those who wish to do so—to make the most of our remaining time and use these last few years wisely.

There are many challenges awaiting us as we age. To the degree that we feel lost in our own small self, separate from others and from spirit, we will find those challenges difficult. To the degree that we are trapped exclusively and unexaminedly in self-referential awareness, in form only, we will live the rest of our days missing the sacred potential of formless awareness, always beckoning, always already here.

The indications for practice offered here present a way to grow in wisdom and peace and connection. They offer an invitation that can call meaningfully to us at this point in our lives, that perhaps can call to us more deeply than ever before. This is an invitation to enter a noble path and finally awaken. All those of us who have, throughout our lives, been stirred even occasionally, even slightly, by such a longing might be able to now receive the invitation with a grateful and timely sense of personal welcome.

AN INVITATION

Because whenever you start the spiritual journey,
the whole of humanity, and perhaps creation,
goes along and shares the journey with you.

—Thomas Keating

WAKE UP

It is time pounding at you, time.
Knowing you are alive
is watching on every side
your generation's short time
falling away as fast as rivers drop though air,
and feeling it hit hard.
—ANNIE DILLARD

BEING OLD IS NEW FOR US.

If we haven't yet come to the recognition that we're old, perhaps we've been lulled by an extended midlife—a new experience in human history. Nevertheless, it's a bit disingenuous of us to pretend that we're not aging, as if all of this could just go on forever, as the unexamined assumptions of our ordinary minds would lull us into believing. Perhaps there's a bit of denial, perhaps a sense of the specialness of "me" that allows me alone exclusion from the river of time.

We surely have gone through the recognition that our youth has ended. We can often pinpoint it to a moment or an event or a year.

It may have come in the form of a loss or a swift visual blow from a mirror or a simple recognition one day that most of the people around us are younger than we are. For many, this recognition prompted a scramble for the relief of that midlife angst: a new car, a new relationship, a renovation, new hair, a facelift, a retreat.

As sobering as it may have been to recognize that our youth has ended, it seems even more difficult for us to recognize that now our midlife is over as well. We've spent our entire life thinking of the aging as "others." It comes as a bit of a shock to realize that we've joined the ranks.

We have growing evidence and indications that others view us as old. We also have a growing recognition of the signs of aging within these bodies of ours. We are, perhaps, not quite so spry. We are, perhaps, not quite so unscarred. Our recognition of our aging beyond midlife may have been heralded by the trials of illness or the impacts of impairments. For some, it's the deep anguish of the care or the loss of a loved one. For others, the recognition can arise from a transition as seemingly benign as retirement or as seemingly insignificant as being either ignored or lent a helping hand by one of the billions who is younger than we are.

Our generation's short time is falling away. We're moving into new terrain.

There is a measure of effort involved in coming to some equanimity with the implications of our own aging. There are the aches and the sags, as we are no longer at the peak of our physical strength and agility. We need, also, to find peace in the new landscape of superfluity, as we no longer are at the peak of our engagement in the world.

Adjusting our views of ourselves can take some time. Adjusting our views of our place in the world and of our further direction can also take some time. The contemplation of these necessary adjustments is meaningful. Our views determine our experience.

New questions emerge, often clamoring for attention. Who am

I beyond the functions I've served? Who am I when the habits of a lifetime are stripped away? Who am I beyond the persona I've presented to the world and to myself? Who am I, bare?

It can be a bit sobering, sometimes even stunning, to realize that there is far less time before us than time behind us. There are fewer full moons whose light we can sit in than full moons whose light we have sat in before. There are fewer pale green springs and autumn's falling leaves, fewer quiet blanketings of snow, fewer ion-charged moments before a fierce summer storm unleashes itself. The times that we will see our children again, having spent every moment with them for the many years of their childhoods, are numbered.

Like our breath, all of the patterned markers of our impermanence are numbered. We're looking at finitude. Aging forces us to look at our shelf life.

We know aging in the aches of muscles and creaks of bones, in the graying of the hair and the wrinkling of the skin, in the squinting to read the small print and the increased attention we must put into simply hearing conversations. We know aging in the bodily systems that just plain don't work quite the way they used to.

We know aging in the losses we experience. There's a growing awareness of death all around us. How many people have we all known by this point in our lives who have died, who have entered a mystery beyond our imagining?

We see our parents die and leave us with no buffer from death. We're next. We lose siblings, our nestlings. We lose friends and cousins, our age peers. Our spouses, our beloveds, our partners die, leaving us stunned and bereft and shorn.

Most of us see the currents in the river but never actually take in what they mean for the boat we're floating in. A good measure of stressful effort can go into avoiding any call to wake up and notice, to see the patterns of impermanence and to acknowledge that the pattern of impermanence is universal. That means us.

We prefer, often, to hide in the familiarity of our unmindfulness, usually having done so for so long that unmindfulness seems like home. The dreaming seems like waking, the sleepwalking like living.

Opening deeply to the truth of our own aging is wise. Opening deeply to the truth of our own impermanence is wise. Although such opening may not come easily at first—we all know how the ego tends to resist vulnerability—it is important to do so if we wish to mindfully use the time remaining to us.

The time horizon has shifted. From this new perspective of all of our years, the future looms foreshortened in our minds. Our sense of a personal narrative extends in a linear progression from "then," the story of our past, to a different "then," our fabrication of our future. From the vantage point of six or more decades, we can clearly see that we have much more "was" to look back on than "will be" to look forward to.

It's tricky terrain. This foreshortened future, as it appears to our minds, leaves far less room and time to maneuver. For most of us, the future has always held the promise of hope. The future was always where happiness might happen. The field of hope is suddenly seen to diminish. There's far less time to choreograph a new outcome.

There is a great deal of searingly honest self-reflection and sometimes emotionally difficult growth work involved in letting go of the unfulfilled dreams of our childhood and youth and midlife. It is a piercing rite of passage for all of us to compare our Photoshopped hopes and dreams with the mug shot of our reality.

Coming to a place of acceptance, of ease and peace, with the way it is and the way we are in our oldest decades is demanding work, to be sure. It is, though, necessary, if we wish to rest and live and die in a peaceful mind, free from the limitations we've endured for so long.

There are important questions to ask ourselves if we wish not to waste these last years of ours. Where have my past habits of body and mind, enacted throughout the decades of my life, led me in terms of peace and happiness? What really matters at this point in my life?

Entering our later decades calls us to look more deeply and more truthfully than we perhaps ever have at what we are doing with these lives of ours. We are face to face with our last chance to experience our lives more fully and more freely, to experience it so much more able to love and give and forgive. Many of us have lived much of our lives as a dress rehearsal, without the sharp mindfulness of opening night. How kind and wise it would be to live these last years in presence, authenticity, and radically simple sanity. If we have any desire to ripen into spiritual maturity—into the abiding experience of the sacred, of all that lies beyond this small self—now is the time.

My friends, let's grow up.
Let's stop pretending we don't know the deal here.
Or if we truly haven't noticed, let's wake up and notice.
Look: Everything that can be lost, will be lost.
It's simple—how could we have missed it for so long?
Let's grieve our losses fully, like ripe human beings,
But please, let's not be so shocked by them.

Let's not act so betrayed,
As though life had broken her secret promise to us.
Impermanence is life's only promise to us,
And she keeps it with ruthless impeccability.
To a child she seems cruel, but she is only wild,
And her compassion exquisitely precise:
Brilliantly penetrating, luminous with truth,
She strips away the unreal to show us the real.

This is the true ride—let's give ourselves to it!
Let's stop making deals for a safe passage:
There isn't one anyway, and the cost is too high.
We are not children anymore.
The true human adult gives everything for what cannot
be lost. . . .

—Jennifer Welwood

PREDICTABLE SUFFERINGS

I am of the nature to grow old.
There is no way to escape growing old.
I am of the nature to have ill health.
There is no way to escape ill health.
I am of the nature to die.
There is no way to escape death.
All that is dear to me and everyone I love are of the
nature to change.
There is no way to escape being separated from them.

—THICH NHAT HANH

SOMEWHERE IN THE MIDST of all these years of ours, virtually every last one of us has experienced at least a few moments pervaded by a deep peace, a sense of union, the complete fulfillment of self-forgetfulness. Even if most of the moments of our lives were lost in the dream of self, of form only, we've all spent some time in presence—the experience of formless awareness.

To forget the self and its pettiness, even for a moment, is liberation from tension, from the perpetual stress of maintaining the self's boundaries. To forget the self and its pettiness is to actually show up, open and embracing, in the present moment's play of form and formlessness.

No matter how much we've shoved it to the back burner for other matters that seemed more pressing at the time, our hunger for awareness greater than this small self, bound by birth and death, can still be ours to fulfill and to experience and to abide in. At this point in our lives, we need to decide if we really want to live and die smaller and more impoverished than we need to be. Are we willing to leave this unimaginably precious gift of a human life unopened?

To look at how we ordinarily hold ourselves, to explore and investigate and examine it, is to see how we resist opening to life just as it is. To begin to explore the depths of our awareness usually involves the recognition of the deception, distortion, and myopic limitation in which we've held our being.

For the most part, we live contracted, defended. We live small and unfree. To be fair, the culture in which we were raised offered virtually no options. This restriction in which we've chosen to live, even if by default, puts a great deal of effort into attempting to deny or ignore the way things are. Many of us often treat the truth as if it were a great inconvenient obstacle looming in the middle of our carefully arranged stage set, something we need to tiptoe around.

We've lived many decades in a bit of a fog, in the denial of impermanence. The implications of our own aging seem threatening to our ordinary view of self, to our unexamined expectations, our unconscious points of perspective. Enmeshed in denial, we've lived in all of the stress—physical, mental, emotional—that is denial's inevitable companion, however deeply we may have tried and may continue to try to numb ourselves.

To live a life of an elder is to ripen into being that is more than simply elderly, more than just old. It involves ripening into clear-eyed acceptance of the way things actually exist. That ripening involves, for each of us, many difficult reckonings in the multifaceted, multidimensional understanding that everything that can be lost will be lost.

If we wish to awaken from this small and limiting dream of self, we need to look at our lives and at our attachments. None of these things that we've worked so hard to possess will last. None of these relationships will last. Either we will die or our loved ones will die. None of these bodies will last. Our somatic systems will fail. Our mental faculties will decrease. We will have sickness and illnesses and disorders and syndromes. Indeed, we probably already have them. Many of them just haven't emerged enough yet for the diagnoses.

We may fear the loss of physical attractiveness, physical strength, and capacity for independence. We may fear the loss of easy acceptance and dignity and respectful recognition. Many fear the very loss of place in a culture that would prefer to eject the aged as a too-vivid reminder of decrepitude and mortality. We may fear the loss of mental agility, glowing health, and the circumstances of our lives as we've become accustomed to them, with their veneer of freedom. We fear these attacks on who we think we are and on what we think we need and on how we want to be perceived. We fear the loss of our illusions of control.

Grey hair and sagginess notwithstanding, many of us still cling childishly to so much that is unreal and inessential. Many of us still cling to reputation, to imagined security, to unexamined habits of attitude and behavior, and to self-image. We have deep aversion to having all of our cherished illusions stripped away by life-in-form's seeming indifference.

We all have reservoirs of fear, some large and some small and subtle, around entering this new terrain of unknown and mystery: our last years. What will aging do to me? To my body? To my mind? Will anyone help me if I become too frail to take care of myself? Will I matter to anyone? Will I be a burden? How will I die?

We do not know. We have no clue what these years will hold for us. We have no clue what will happen tomorrow. The "moment that changed everything" usually arrives unannounced.

The only person who can answer the questions posed by the often painful challenges of aging is the person we will be in the moment we confront those circumstances. The shaping of that person into someone with greater wisdom and equanimity can begin in this moment.

To AWAKEN OUT of our mistaken views, to awaken beyond self, we begin by looking. Looking, we see clearly that our lives and everything to which we are attached are all impermanent phenomena. Our suffering will be in direct proportion to our resistance, to our unwillingness to perceive and accept the reality of impermanence. Every moment of attempting to cling brings stress. When we ignore reality—the very essence of ignorance—reality compensates. The result is *dukkha*—suffering, both slight and overwhelming.

To ripen into an elder, into a being that is more than simply elderly and more than only self, is a deliberate, thoughtful, sustained choice that arises from the intention to see things as they are.

There is much having to do with aging and death that we know conceptually but that we have not yet allowed our hearts to open up to and enfold. There are predictable sufferings. Aging, illness, and death show up in our lives as profound teachers.

> Aging, illness, and death are treasures
> for those who understand them.
> They're Noble Truths, Noble Treasures.
> If they were people,
> I'd bow down to their feet every day.
>
> —AJAAN LEE

THIS LIFE-IN-FORM of ours is a created phenomenon, a phenomenon dependent upon conditions. It is impermanent.

There was, at the time of our conception, a coming together of absolutely immeasurable causes and conditions. Among those causes and conditions were the thousands of other moments of conception of every ancestor. They allowed the appearance of this body, this mind, this being. As Linda Hogan, a Native American writer, observes, "You are the result of the love of thousands." For those of us in these last chapters of our life, perhaps only one or two of the beings whose conception was a cause of our own are left. All the rest have vanished. This life-in-form is mortal.

Ninety-nine percent of the species that ever existed on our planet are extinct. Any causes and conditions that come together also come apart. We've always, on some level, understood that. We can see the rise and fall of a flower, of fads, of seasons, of storms and empires, of lovebugs and climates and galaxies. We do not have a similar clarity of view about the rise and fall, the appearance and the dissolution, of ourselves.

We have always viewed the path of human development as one that arises with dependency. We have forgotten or dismissed or ignored the recognition that it also often ends in dependency, a dependency arising from diminishment.

The dependency at the beginning of life-in-form is deemed "cute" and endearing. It attracts us. Those big eyes of a child can ensure a lot of leeway. We view the life course as passing through a long, ascending period of seeming independence and agency, belts notched with whatever accomplishments we designate as mattering. The now-prolonged period of middle adulthood that we experience in this century is held, in many ways, as the height of a human life.

And, after that "height," we view the life course as falling away from the apex, as if degenerating, declining, quite often into some form of dependence again. This time, however, the dependence is viewed as anything but cute. It does not attract.

We sometimes hold our aging state, clearer to all with each passing day, with embarrassment or awkwardness or unease. Many choose to secrete themselves away with equally wrinkled others. The younger observers sometimes hold those of us in this seeming decline or second dependency at arm's length. Many try to spare themselves the view of their own future.

Diapers to diapers. That's the nature of the curve. And then, on that continuum of a human life, comes death, the end of life-in-form. Dust to dust.

We've always known that this is the course of a human life. We just have not put our sense of "me" into the equation. Many of us act betrayed and affronted and certainly humbled when we are forced to recognize that impermanence also applies to us.

Our culture is the provider of most of the thoughts and attitudes of our ordinary minds. The culture's view tends to hold the long period of seeming independence and agency, filled with hope and promise and often untouched by tragedy, as the exemplar of a human being. Without examining our assumption, most of us have held the decades of our thirties, forties, and fifties, possibly even our sixties, as the gauge of a worthy human life.

Somehow, those of us who have aged, who have—willingly or unwillingly—moved beyond active participation in the world of midlife, are viewed as "less than" or irrelevant. At times, we hold this view as well. We experience sadness and fear and some disorientation in this view. Without a deeper context, a spiritual context or orientation beyond self, with which to view and to hold this whole experience of a human existence, aging is something most of us would not choose, something to simply endure.

We have become very used to dismissing the importance of the last years of our lives, because they do not measure up to the criteria of midlife. The old are measured by midlife values.

If we are to claim the last years of life as years that hold the possibility of awakening into equanimity and lightness, into the very embodiment of grace, we need to bear witness to the ripening of that possibility. Not only would it be a blessing for each of us, it would be a blessing for a world starving for such witnessing.

We can choose to bear witness to the grace in aging. Doing so, we can reveal the profound and noble value of the wise use of this time. The attainments of minds of peace, compassion, and sanity, the fruits of committing our last years to awakening, have very little to do with the cultural standards of success at midlife.

To AWAKEN, we want to look at where we resist looking. In addition to fear of the loss of independence and relevance, fear of appearance deemed conventionally unattractive, and fear of increased fragility and decline, it's mainly our fears of death and dying that keep us from opening our hearts deeply to the experience of our own aging. It's primarily our fear of the end of "me" that keeps us attempting to overlook the reality of our own advancing years and our declining physical body.

We need to be able to wrap our heads around our own mortality. It is helpful to let go of all that binds us far before the hour of our death. This will not decrease our love for all the dear ones in our lives. At the moment, many of us have confused loving with grasping and craving, with attachment and some sense of neediness. To let go of all that binds us allows us to love more and to love more widely and to love with far greater generosity.

Letting go while in the midst of life is helpful to avoid profound psychological anguish at the time of dying. Letting go of all that binds us while still in the midst of life allows our experience of ripening in spirit, with all of the grace inherent in that ripening, long before we die.

Fearful of depth, largely because most of us have kept it so unknown, we have spent a long time uneasily skating over the surface of life. Deepened awareness and recognition of our impermanence, quite simply, can provide the urgency to want to let go of all of the stress and confusion, the suffering large and small, of living on the surface.

Our mistaken sense of separate self generates fear. The experience of fear arises inevitably with the conviction of separation. We can ask ourselves how much have we given up because of fear? How have we tried to protect ourselves from all that is threatening to who we believe ourselves to be, from all that is outside whatever small comfort zone we've created for ourselves? How has it felt to live in this degree of defendedness? Everything we long for is beyond the wall of fear.

For most of us, most of the time, we engage in denial, defensiveness, and contractive reactivity. These habits are ones of tightening and limiting. They simmer in the chronic low-level anxiety of the self. This the Buddha unflinchingly labeled "ignorance." Our ignorance is maintained in our refusal to look deeply, unflinchingly.

Most of us do not yet know our own essential nature. Maybe we can feel the pain of limitation and the unease of contraction and the longing for liberation beyond self, but we cling to what's familiar. We are like a chick, afraid to break through the ever-so-thin shell of the already outgrown and painfully confining egg.

Our small little ego will not save us from the predictable sufferings of aging and death. It has no strategies, no power. It offers no refuge.

It is wise to come to know our own depths, to plumb and explore them, to allow our hearts to break open, to allow our minds to investigate that which they would rather deny, to allow ourselves to contemplate impermanence, to take death in—our own and the deaths of all of those we love.

Having entered the terrain beyond midlife, aging and death are the aspects of the continuum of a human life we are now called upon to experience. It is our turn. We've done infancy and toddlerhood, years and years of schooling. We've done the golden time of coming of age and experiencing the heady joys of young sexuality and new ideas and new freedoms. We've done the household years; the money-making, accomplishing years; and the time of planning for retirement. Now, it's our turn to face the fading and the ending of our own fleeting appearance.

To contemplate dying each day brings forth a view with more wisdom. It reorients us and keeps us moving in the right direction, toward deeper wisdom and into greater love. To contemplate dying each day calls forth an instant reordering of priorities. Just like a quick and deliberate shake of a kaleidoscope, it creates a whole new patterning, a whole new view. Most of us need to be shaken out of our complacency.

If we were to take to heart the fact of our fleeting and precarious existence, would we really continue all of our worldly striving and consuming? Would we really be upset about the same things today that upset us yesterday? How many of our grudges and disappointments would still seem important? Would we continue to have unhealed relationships? Would we still leave the words of gratitude and of forgiveness and of love unspoken? How would we greet each wondrous being that engages in connection with us? How would we live each day differently?

Lost in what seems like comfort, the vast majority of us have allowed our unexamined attitudes to live our lives for us. And the more we allow our habitual mental and emotional habits to remain unexamined, the more we continue to grasp on to the illusory belief in the small, separate self that identifies with those habits.

Unless we question with the intention to see, our experience of life continues and will continue, stressed and embroiled. When we remain in the confines of selfing, we're like the drowning animal that gets stuck in an eddy. All else flows with the clear and aerated stream, effortlessly and with ease, but the animal just keeps getting battered with whatever other debris lands in the same backwater. It keeps getting beaten, over and over, against the same rocks.

We can intend to use these last years with skill and meaning, seizing the essence of this precious human life.

Mindful of impermanence, the breath-by-breath arising and abiding and falling of each moment, we can remain in remembrance of our longing to exist in wisdom and love and compassion. We can remain in our intention to ripen into the spiritual maturity that is our birthright to cultivate. There is no more noble way to spend these years than to become an elder, to bear witness to the world as placeholders for peace, love, wisdom, and fearlessness.

Contemplation of our death provides the urgency that keeps us aware that this moment right now, this opportunity to enter the timeless present, is passing. We begin to imprint the truth of impermanence at a deep level with a breath-by-breath acknowledgment.

Impermanence does not occur only in reference to decades or years or weeks or days. Impermanence is the nature of every arising moment. Each precious moment matters. It has never arisen before. It will never return again.

Opening to the reality of our own death, we deepen our determination to wring the most out of every moment of opportunity, every now that this human experience offers.

Contemplating death can lead to a humbling, grateful acceptance of our own moment-by-moment fragility, of this miraculous confluence of the immeasurable causes and conditions that give rise to and sustain a human life. That we still breathe, that the heart still pumps blood, that our sense organs can still contact light and sound and touch and taste and smell, that it all still works, is dazzling.

How precious an opportunity to experience this ephemeral condition, as fragile as a water bubble, with its rare potential for awakening. We want to grow wonder, humility, gratitude.

Looking deeply, we're hit with the truth that the heart pumps blood, that our sense organs contact light and sound and touch and taste and smell, that our lungs breathe, that food is metabolized and cells nourished, all by themselves. They simply occur. They occur by themselves, as long as the appropriate causes and conditions remain. Imagine if it had been our responsibility all along to keep the breath going. We'd already be dead. We would have forgotten to inhale the next breath a long time ago.

The processes of the body, with which we so identify and to which we are so attached, are utterly impersonal. We may feel ourselves to be the possessor of these processes but they are unownable and beyond our grasp. And, we can ask, who is there to own them?

In the same way, our thoughts and emotions, such convincing evidence of "me" and of "my views," occur as organic processes. They simply arise as long as the appropriate causes and conditions remain. They arise by themselves. They're not personal. Just think of all of the thoughts and feelings that have arisen today, like swarms of mosquitoes, out of the blue. They arise by themselves, from habituated familiarity, deeply ingrained neural firings.

Although we've identified with the experiences of our body, our senses, our emotions, and our thoughts for all of these decades, we have mistaken impersonal processes for who we are. Doing so, we've become attached to this meaty body, finely tuned to any potential harm to this tender and vulnerable flesh. We've become attached to our own familiar emotions, often allowing them to run our days and decades as if they knew what they were doing. We've become attached to our thoughts and assumptions, often willing to harm ourselves and others, in subtle and not so subtle ways, for the sake of our opinions and judgments and reputations.

Having mistaken impersonal processes for who we are, we've

blocked our own access to the vaster awareness in which these processes occur. Most of us feel, when we really reflect, confined in self. We *are* confined in self.

We are all capable of carving out greater depth, more spaciousness. When we open ourselves to the fragility of this body and the impersonal nature of the organic processes of this body and mind, we deepen our appreciation of each single wondrous moment of this life of ours. Deepening our appreciation, we increase our presence and our ease.

Causes and conditions have come together. Causes and conditions will come apart.

Deepening our clarity as to what really matters allows us to let go of the energy caught in reactivity toward all those beings and circumstances that don't even exist in the way we believe them to exist. What ease, liberation, and newly released energetic awareness, trapped and squandered mindlessly for so long, lie in that letting go. This deepened and sharpened awareness will be invaluable in the challenges of later years.

THERE ARE PREDICTABLE sufferings in a human life: birth, aging, death, not getting what we want, getting what we don't want, and the impossibility of finding permanent satisfaction in the universe of self. We cannot avoid these. Each of us has experienced many of them already, no matter who we are, no matter how wealthy or healthy or loved, no matter how well-guarded the doors or the gates of the subdivision.

We double the suffering of each by relating to it reactively. Everything about the nature of our own experience with these predictable sufferings lies in the inner stance with which we meet them. Will we allow the same old habits of our selfing to hijack these precious, later years as well? Will we meet whatever challenges or diminishments arise with countless further attempts to deny or manipulate? Or the attention-grabbing drain of victimhood? The bitterness of self-pity or the paralysis of bewilderment?

We double the suffering of a human life by the suffering we assume—literally take upon ourselves—in our reactions to the predictable sufferings. There is pain and there is sickness. There is disappointment; there is loss. Those are all unavoidable in a human life. The degree of suffering we experience is determined by our relationship to pain and sickness and disappointment and loss. We double the suffering of a human life with our attachments and aversions, our lack of equanimity and our lack of wisdom about the way things actually exist. We magnify it; we live in "suffering squared."

What are we afraid we might lose, if we let go, if we stepped out of the comfort zone of selfing into the unbounded freedom of the sacred, for which we have always hungered? It's important to look because these are the places where we are bound in our own smallness, our own fears. These are the places where we will stay bound without mindfulness.

Emergence beckons. Life is waiting for us.

OPENING, ALLOWING, LETTING go, we increase the chances of freeing our awareness to enter into a timeless present, beyond self. Beyond self is beyond fear. As for fear and self, they are inseparable. With eyes open, who would choose to keep awareness bound in an illusory self with a short shelf life?

Even those of us with a longing to awaken oftentimes find ourselves caught between that longing and our fears. Caught here, we can get paralyzed or bewildered or discouraged or lulled back to sleep by the seeming complacency of denial. If we have any desire to awaken, this is our last chance. As Je Tsongkhapa, a realized Tibetan lama, said centuries ago, "This is no time to sleep, you fools!"

CREATING THE CAUSES

To enter an awakened dimension
often means living within its rules
prior to awakening to its truths.

—RODNEY SMITH

STEPPING ONTO THE NOBLE PATH

> Geese appear high over us,
> pass, and the sky closes. Abandon,
> as in love or sleep, holds
> them to their way, clear
> in the ancient faith: what we need
> is here. And we pray, not
> for new earth or heaven, but to be
> quiet in heart, and in eye
> clear. What we need is here.
>
> —WENDELL BERRY

IT IS AN INCREDIBLE MOMENT in the life of a human being, a turning point of boundless importance, when the percentages of the wish to awaken and the wish to continue sleepwalking shift from fifty/fifty to fifty-one/forty-nine. May we all reach the point where, as Anais Nin put it, "the risk to remain tight in the bud was more painful than the risk it took to blossom." At that point, we enter a noble path.

The spiritual path, in essence, is one of recognizing and then diminishing the difference between our spiritual aspirations and whatever spiritual understanding we have developed, on one hand, and where we actually live in our day-to-day consciousness, on the other. We want these two hands to meet, together, with no space between them, in the perpetual prayer of a mind that is peacefully present.

Just as walking sticks and other necessities may help us on a long trek—especially at our age—there are certain necessities for a spiritual journey. And just as a hiker on foot can't wish him or herself from the beginning to the end of the Appalachian Trail or the Camino de Santiago, we can't wish ourselves awakened and free.

To arrive at what is already here, we need intention and commitment and a practice that will enable the heart to be quiet and the eye to be clear.

Intention is developed in radically honest self-reflection, piercing to the deepest of our heart's longings. Intention arises from our hunger and opens to our fulfillment.

But although intention is a necessary factor, clearly we do not awaken simply because we wish to awaken. We maintain and strengthen our intention in the simplicity and discipline of commitment, which immerses us in the intention to awaken. It brings the intention to life, our life. Commitment and intention feed each other. We can rely on this truth.

There are certain other catalysts that we can bring together that will serve our intention, catalysts that function causally to effect awakening. As we go about finding and/or deepening a path and intensifying our commitment to practice, we would do well to conceive of this gathering of catalysts as simply creating the causes that allow awakening to unfold as it will unfold.

We do this mindfully. Striving to awaken is the action of self-cherishing and will keep us trapped. Ego's strategies are incapable of moving beyond ego. To create the causes of awakening, on the other hand, is the wise action of a lightly-held functioning self, spurred by an essential longing.

Gathering and enabling these catalysts doesn't mean we need to change the circumstances of our lives, necessarily; we simply need to insert the causes of transformation into them. We are wise to bring intention, a committed practice, and support for our direction into our remaining years.

Choosing a time-honored path orients us toward awakening. It allows us to have some sense of confidence before we have developed genuine confidence in life's invitation to us and in our growing capacity to accept the invitation. We choose a path that resonates with us, or we strengthen our resonance within a path that we have already chosen. Every authentic path offers a practice.

A committed, formal sitting practice is essential if we wish to awaken. It is possible to call ourselves spiritual travelers, to believe that we are on a spiritual path, even to become kinder and wiser human beings without a daily sitting practice. It is not likely, though, that we will awaken into awareness beyond self and ripen all of our positive potentialities without a contemplative, meditative discipline. Although there seem to have been cases of spontaneous awakening, it's probably best not to count on one.

We're fooling ourselves a bit to think that we're meditating as we're gardening or walking or out on the golf course or volunteering or even reading "spiritual books." Those are all causes and conditions that, with the right mindset—a mindset based on wise intention and anchored to a committed sitting practice—can enable us to relax, to be more at peace, to have some insights, to even have an occasional experience of oneness with all that is. But those activities, in and of themselves, without anchoring in strong intention and a committed sitting practice, are unable to transform and free our minds. They are not, in themselves, the necessary causes of awakening. Let's not deceive ourselves in the time we have left.

> In theory there is no difference between theory and practice.
> In practice there is.
> —YOGI BERRA

We need the focused, concentrated energy of awareness that seems only to be cultivated with a daily practice if we wish to walk through the world with clarity and compassion. We need to carve out the time to sit if we have not yet done so, or carve out more time if we have already begun. Sitting—the silent, noble stilling of the body and the mind for the purpose of liberating awareness into beyond-self, into deeper, more illumined consciousness—allows an opening in the limited, limiting paradigm of separate self and only form.

Sitting practice is where transformation is effected, where neural connections are rewired. Sitting practice is the launching pad for piercing insight, direct knowing, and the opening of the heart. It is the base of operations.

THROUGH COMMITTED PRACTICE we can become increasingly confident that we have the skillful means to sustain our growth and transformation through all that arises as we age. A friend in his late sixties commented, "We're heading down the slippery slope. There's less and less time to practice."

For some of us, predictable sufferings have already arisen. The list of losses and diminutions grows. For those of us whose lives have the appearance of being untouched by aging so far, it is not helpful to think "if" predictable sufferings arise for me. The real wake-up call lies in recognizing that it is only a matter of "when" they will arise.

We need a practice of looking at our own minds. There is no

other way for our minds to become unbound. This is an experience only we can give ourselves. No book or thought or teacher or saint or bodhisattva can give it to us, much as we might wish this were so. It might take longer than we have left to us to come up with the same dazzling sophistication of transformative practices that every wisdom tradition offers at its innermost core. At this point in our lives, without fifty years languidly stretching before us as has been the case earlier, it seems wise to work with what has been proven and time-honored.

We need a practice that we can sustain and that will sustain us during all that we will encounter. We don't know what lies in the future for each of us. We would do well to enter the transformative process, to jump into the deep end of the pool, now, while we have relative strength and mental agility. We would do well to cultivate stability and clarity, the courage of presence, while we have the luxury of some relatively peaceful opportunity.

How would we practice through dialysis or radiation or repeated surgeries and other violations of tender flesh? Could we keep a peaceful mind? How would we practice through the often impersonal indifference of a nursing home, waiting for someone to wash us or feed us? How would we practice through the impairments of a stroke? Could we keep a loving mind without falling into old reactive patterns and getting trapped back in them?

Would we be able to access a peaceful mind and sustain it through the endless and sometimes thankless demands of caregiving? Caregiving is often a 24/7 job demanded of us when our physical energy is depleting and our emotional resources stretched. Would we be able to stay present, to simply be, with the one who needs care? Would we be able to offer him or her all of the love and compassion that we would wish for ourselves and that we would wish to give?

What would sustain us through senility or dementia? Would anything? What would we want to be our last deliberate thought?

Will we be able to sustain the equanimity that would allow us to remain nonreactive to the arisings of our own ramblings?

Such scenarios do not just happen to others. For so long, many of us have often thought of people as falling into one of two groups—people were either "sick" or "healthy." At some point, we need to stop and think, if the circumstances of our lives have not already forced us to do so, that many people in the "sick" group were in the "healthy" group yesterday.

We need a practice that can sustain us through whatever arises from now until our last breath. We need the awareness and realizations that arise from such a noble practice, awareness and realizations that will sustain us in grace.

Both a noble path and a transformative practice focus our attention. The noble path, adopted through intention, is the directive factor. The practice is the transformative factor.

The practice is the mold in which we can tame the habituated patterns of uncontrolled mind and the sense of self they give rise to. The practice is the crucible for the alchemy; it allows awakening to unfold.

The awakened state is already here, already now. It is only our ceaseless self-reference that blocks our recognition of this and our experience of it. Our ceaseless self-reference is our most deeply-ingrained habit pattern. It is foundational in our psyche, hard-wired for survival. It is also replete with countless other deeply ingrained habit patterns, formed in the repetitive thoughts and actions and reactions of these many years of ours. Each of these habit patterns has kept us mistakenly grasping to a will-o'-the-wisp. Each has kept us asleep, lost in a dream and far from the light of here and now.

It is sobering but it is true: our habit patterns will continue as they always have without the application of the mindfulness developed in a practice. We will recreate endless variations of the same scenarios with the same emotional reactions, over and over.

Occasionally we may have wondered about the feeling of déjà vu, when we have the exact same argument with a spouse or a sibling or a child, when we feel slighted or misunderstood or ripped off for the thousandth time, when we return to a familiar emotional shade of disappointment or despair or ennui or overwhelm.

We may have wondered whether or not we may have a part in the reappearing scenarios and the well-known reactions. Mostly, though, without the mindfulness developed in a practice, we use our conclusions from each new similar scenario to further bolster the very conclusions that created it.

Just as we did in our twenties, thirties, and forties, we will harbor the same reactive patterns in our sixties, seventies, and eighties unless we intend otherwise and unless we commit to a transformative practice that can enable us to realize our intention to awaken.

To AWAKEN INTO clarity and sanity, to allow a mind of peace, we sit. We sit with a mind intent upon seeing what is essential. To see what is essential, we carve out what is inessential.

We carve out the busy-ness and distractions that often occupy our day and create the space and time for a spiritual practice. Actually, the fact that we *are* old and have slowed down anyway is of great benefit. Busy-ness can take a toll on mindfulness.

Sitting in mindfulness, we carve out some of our resistances to awakening. We increase our willingness to dissipate the obstructions, the unexamined but nevertheless seductive contents of our own mind's habits. These habits block the experience of grace, the experience of our own essential nature, beyond self and beyond form. Sitting in mindfulness, we create the space in our heart for intention and commitment and earnestness to plant themselves and begin to flourish.

To mindfully observe the thoughts and urges and accompanying emotions and stories of our habitual patterns of mind is a bit like observing the smudges on a sliding glass door. We see where we need to work to eliminate the smudges, to diminish the obstructions these habitual patterns and usual identifications place on any clear view of our essential nature.

When we enter a noble path and practice within it, the insights of wisdom begin to replace our habitual mistaken conceptions. As our own peace and fulfillment grow, the heart naturally opens and wishes such equanimity for all beings in our suffering world. Our intention for liberation from attachment to self overflows and holds that wish for all beings still assailed by the waves of selfing. We, with committed practice, widen our view to remember and include others. Our wish to bear witness to all that lies beyond self intensifies. This is compassion growing.

To INSTITUTE a daily practice, we need to know what we're doing as we sit to meditate. We definitely need to know what we're doing as our practice deepens, as our capacity to enter absorption grows. It is immeasurably helpful to have a teacher, in much the same way that climbers who attempt to encounter the Himalayan mountains need a *sherpa*, a knowledgeable guide. Put your foot here, not there. Watch out for the ten thousand foot drop over the precipice.

There are subtleties abounding as we go deeper and deeper into absorbed and concentrated states of awareness. We want to make sure we negotiate the twists and turns as skillfully as possible. We want to stay open and gratefully receptive to the gift of wise and loving counsel. The counsel of someone who has gone before us and has already cleared his or her mind, in large measure, from self-reference is immeasurably helpful.

There are some sand traps on the course. And, for a very long way, the persistent little ego can easily sneak in for the ride, hijacking the golf cart. It seems to prefer heading right for the sand traps, often even while posturing a suitably "spiritual" demeanor. It is helpful to receive guidance from those who know the course.

Checking in periodically with someone who we can recognize as having gone further along the path than we have is helpful. We are fortunate beyond imagining to live and to age in a time when there are many who are worthy of the honorific "teacher." One test of the worthiness of that honorific is that such a person has no desire other than to share with others what has been shared with him or her, simply to help them awaken, to pass along the kindness.

To become an elder, more than simply elderly, we need a daily practice based on careful and carefully understood instructions. It is our good fortune that such instructions are ample in our time.

At many times in the world, such was not the case. Even now, in many parts of the world, there is no access to a teacher whatsoever, much less the degree of access we in our culture have to a few thousand qualified teachers from every tradition—available in person, in books, and online. We are incredibly fortunate beings to meet the Dharma and the noble practices of Dharma in all the expressions they take, both Eastern and Western.

It is also immeasurably helpful to have others in our lives with whom we can share our intentions and experiences from time to time. It is of great benefit to have at least a few others who have carved out a similar degree of depth in their being and share the same longing. We can support each other in our shared and noble purpose. We learn from each other's unfolding, speaking together easily and flowingly of subtleties and intentions that are rarely spoken in other circles.

This is the incredible value of *sangha*, of spiritual friends. Pierre Teilhard de Chardin, the French Catholic mystic, describes this wish for sangha beautifully, as almost a sensual longing for others with an equally vast vision. They can help us point out the blind spots of our ego, our self-deceptions that continue for such a long time.

OUR OWN EGOS keep us from all that lies beyond self in every moment. A spiritual practice isn't about killing the ego, though. It's about letting go of our attachment to it, letting go of our eagerness to count it as real and important, our eagerness to stay lost in its seduction, our eagerness, even, for it to be awakened, illuminated.

But the self doesn't get liberated. The self is what awareness gets liberated from. A spiritual practice enables us to transcend self with a deeper and expanded awareness that includes and informs and illuminates self, allowing it to function in the world as a vehicle for spirit.

A spiritual practice isn't about becoming good or saintly or boring or a doormat. It's not really about becoming anything. It's just about being, allowing being. It's simply about allowing our awareness to be unfettered, to be released from its patterns of ignorance, so that it naturally blossoms into fruition. It's about letting go, relaxing, easing into being. Most of us have spent many a decade without the contentment of complete and utter ease.

A noble practice enables us to increase our awareness of the nitty-gritty of our experience of life, replete with every fabrication and drama and obstruction and reactivity and snag. We, over time, develop the capacity to remain in equanimity in the face of whatever arises. On a noble path, over time, we change the locus of our identity from the contents of our awareness to awareness itself, always already a state of grace.

A spiritual practice enables a decrease in the "Dharma lag": the time passing between the arising of a thought, a word, a behavior, an attitude, and the clear and mindful awareness of the arising. Sadly, we may have Dharma lags that are fifty or sixty years old. It is certainly possible, with practice and with intention, to decrease the lag time. With that growing diminution of the Dharma lag, we begin to be in the present moment, the arising and the recognition occurring simultaneously. We can begin to experience the completeness, the wholeness, the refuge of presence as it unfolds each arising appearance.

We may have stalled in whatever spiritual aspirations we've had earlier in our lives, waiting for the right time or for someone to point out the way. But the time is now and the way is right here. Walking the path is simply a matter of showing up. We just begin looking, exploring where we are in our mindbody and what is actually happening in this moment. Then, we explore where we are and what is actually happening in the next moment, and then where we are and what is actually happening in the moment after that, the next unfolding of now.

This is mindfulness—intended, open, noninterfering attention placed on each moment's arising. Mindfulness is developed in the practices of every valid path. Applying that mindfulness allows the tiniest bit of distance, of dis-identification, from our familiar assumptions and reactivities. Our own karmic habit patterns become more manageable, more malleable, more transparent. We realize that we have options. The mindful recognition of option, this particular opening of seeing a moment of choice and allowing the wisdom of awareness to discern the most beneficial view, enables transformation.

This adoption of a noble path and a transformative practice, the engines of a transformative process, is one in which we mix our intention's wisdom into karma's unconscious patternings. That addition of the discerning wisdom of wise intention, available moment by moment, takes where we are in one moment and changes the course of the next moment. It releases energy that had been trapped in the patterns that limited awareness. This energy is freed from the same old karmic imprints and can unfold into the next moment with more wisdom.

We can shape a new trajectory with the creativity of intention and the discriminating eye of mindfulness. We want to aim toward love and compassion and wisdom, the qualities that flow from unfettered awareness and invited us into that awareness to begin with.

With our intention as the tip of the arrow, all of our energies follow suit in the trajectory of the arc.

We can see this in any situation in our lives. If our intention has been to accumulate money, our days and our attention and our decisions and our effort and our sense of worth were constructed in such a way as to hold the bag to catch the coins. Now we find that we're not quite at home in all our newly nonmonetized moments. If our intention has been to be found attractive, we will have noticed all of the eyes that were willing to flirt and admire. These days, no longer admired as so physically attractive by the cultural standards and the instincts for mating, our self-worth may have a rough time in these older years. If our intention was to fortify a shaky sense of self by feeling needed, we will have constructed a life designed to help us feel indispensable, filled with stray puppies and others in need of our rescuing. To no longer have the stamina to be universally indispensable may rock our world.

We would do well to ask ourselves what motivations were allowed to run these lives of ours. We have created much of the warp and woof of our life, its daily rhythms and the touchstones of ego, from our unmindful intentions.

In the same way—although with infinitely greater potency because of the depth from which the intention arises—if our intention is to awaken, we weave a new experience of being. We begin to live every moment as part of the awakening experience. This intention is an immeasurably wise cause to create, to heed with fidelity and to hold in gratitude.

A MAP OF AWAKENING

> Let there be
> an opening
> into the quiet
> that lies beneath
> the chaos,
> where you find
> the peace
> you did not think
> possible
> and see what shimmers
> within the storm.
>
> —Jan Richardson

Setting out on a noble path, it is helpful to have a map of the terrain of awakening. We want to find the opening into the quiet.

Maps of new territory expand our paradigms, our worldviews. They can pry open some tightly held horizons. We want our paradigms to be porous, our fabrications to be held lightly. Perhaps we've hardened our opinions and beliefs as we've aged, but we've all had the experience of an open mind, eager to expand its horizons. If we have not had that experience often, we can cultivate it. Freedom is always dancing on the perimeter, inviting us out into it.

We need just a wee bit of courage to follow our longing, to leave the familiar and set out on a journey.

Centuries of human beings expanded their views of the known world through exploration. Each explorer left maps for others to follow—whether it be to the river on the other side of the mountain or through the terrain of the Silk Road or across the vast ocean to the shock of a new continent. We're still doing it: maps of galaxies and quadrants of the cosmos. The explorers and mapmakers lay out the terrain, reveal the passages of the journey. Each bit of newly mapped territory expands the horizons of those who even view the maps.

In the same way, if we choose to use these older years to awaken, a map of the territory is essential to expand what we hold as possible, to point out the way. So far, most of us have only navigated form. With our attention virtually trapped in form, we've missed an entire half of the universe—the formless, always already here.

The territory of awakening has been explored and mapped just as has the world of form. Each wisdom tradition offers such a map, a way of viewing spiritual growth, which expands our horizons and informs our understanding of the journey. The map won't track the path each of us takes individually, but it provides an overview of the landscape of increasingly more subtle and less obstructed levels of awareness and can serve as a general guide.

To CHOOSE a spiritual path is to adopt a view of the process of awakening. That view allows the path to be spoken of in a way that our conceptual mind, the mind in which we all begin to walk a spiritual path, can grasp.

The overview understanding of a path, the map of it, is a skillful means. In all likelihood, it will be superseded by progressively clearer, more precise, more inclusive understandings until clear wisdom dawns, the direct and unmediated experience of knowing. Clear wisdom is possible for each and every one of us; each of us holds this potential to go beyond mere conceptualization and the need for maps.

There are probably thousands of constructs that attempt to describe the dynamics of transformation. They comprise the views, the realized perspectives, of those who have practiced any of the world's wisdom traditions, all pathways home. Although each map or overview may be slightly different, all use an avenue of the truth, an angle of the truth, to help us clear our own way home, back to our essential nature.

There really is only one Dharma. It's a Buddhist term, but Buddhists don't own it. *Dharma* simply means the truth as realized awareness and as path to that realized awareness.

All wisdom traditions recognize the necessity of freeing our attention from self-reference. A predominant aspect of almost all of the constructs of all of the paths, both Western and Eastern, is the theme of transformation, of awakening, occurring in the act of surrender, the laying down of the self.

The laying down of the self can occur in literally billions of ways. It can occur only in each of our individual journeys. For each of us, it will have a slightly different look to it or slightly different view steering it—a slightly different access approach, according to our individual patterns, our karma, and the interpretation of different teachings. We all resonate differently. Even so, the recognition of the self as a limiting, binding locus of identification, followed by the laying down of the self, is a rite of passage in all wisdom traditions. We lay down the attachment to self and the illusion of self, releasing all that previously trapped and congested energy into ever-present awareness.

One of the most moving understandings of the laying down of self is represented in the Ten Oxherding Pictures from the Zen tradition: block prints that depict the spiritual path of mastering one's own mind through the metaphor of a young man seeking to tame a wild ox. In the eighth picture of a series of ten, the journeyer is beckoned to enter the void, the space of beyond-self. The space is open and calling to the journeyer, the yearner, to follow the path of those who have already awakened.

The eighth picture in this series is beautifully represented as an empty circle—both the ox and the oxherder have been transcended. Clearly, the congested nature, the seeming solidity, of the small, separate, contracted self-sense cannot enter into the subtle clear light of this emptiness.

Most of us have some work to do to enable entry into that opening. We can think: how many of the moments of this day have I spent thinking about "I" and "me" and "mine"? How many moments wondering how each arising circumstance affects me? How many moments resting in the blind conviction that each unexamined, arising belief supports my sense of me? How much clinging and aversion, contraction and lack of ease lie trapped in this tense congestion?

Most of us have dug deep trenches of stress and unease. It is truly now or never in terms of letting go of this tight hold on self. If we do not do it now, death will do it for us and we will have missed the dazzlingly grace-filled life that was offered to us.

The laying down of the self, the letting go of attachment to self, is our biggest challenge. It is fraught with fear, defensiveness, resistance. This seems to be so regardless of the wisdom tradition in which we are practicing. Selfing is deeply ingrained in all of us.

For some, even the common English renditions "emptiness" and "void" of the Sanskrit word *sunyata* are frightening, so attached are we to form. *Sunyata* derives from the Sanskrit word for *zero*. Zero is not negative, not nothing—an empty, meaningless, nonexistent. Nor is zero positive; it is not something—an inherently existent form. Zero is the still point where form and formless meet in perfect balance. This is the awakened state. To live at the zero point is to live liberated.

Like the medieval cartographers of Europe, who felt one would fall into endless space at the edges of the oceans of their maps, we fear the presumed nothingness of no-self. Fortunately, there have been many spiritual circumnavigators, such as the Oxherding fellow, who have returned to tell the tale of the beauty beyond self.

IN BUDDHIST WISDOM, much steadfast effort goes into developing the stability of mind that allows insight into the insubstantiality, the ephemerality, of the self. The recognition of not-self, *anatta*, the unfindability of the self that we think we are, is the door to liberation.

This same laying down of the self occurs using the injunction from the example Jesus set: "Not my will, but Thy will be done." The practice here, within Christian contemplative traditions, is one of entering, through committed and surrendered waves of ever-deeper openings, into a silent, receptive mindstate of prayer, of communion. This is the prayer of quiet, the prayer of the heart. Ego is not present in this deepest of intimacies; it cannot enter the *sanctum sanctorum*.

This laying down of self, awakening from a myopic dream of existence bounded by self, does not in any way imply that a functioning self is no longer needed in a human existence. We still need to pay the electric bill, tie our shoes, and stop at a traffic light. We still need a self with which we can function and through which the grace of flowering potentialities can shine. Formlessness functions through form.

The tenth of the ten pictures in the Zen Oxherding series is of the journeyer returned, radiant and smiling, to share this presence, awareness beyond self, in the marketplace. We need a functioning self as the vehicle for engaging—lovingly, compassionately, and wisely—as an elder, with others and with the world.

To recognize the need for a functioning self is not the same as believing in the reality of that self as the shining glory of our potential.

We are so caught and small and deluded in the minds of self-cherishing and self-grasping. We can define self-cherishing as the secretly harbored belief all egos have that my happiness is more important than anyone else's. Thank goodness we cannot yet hear each other's thoughts. Thank goodness others cannot yet hear all of ours. Self-cherishing is the foolish preference for one mental image, my mental image of "me," over another mental image, my mental image of "you."

We can define self-grasping as imputing, constructing, and clinging in attachment to a separate, localized sense of self, existing as mere concept, yet laden with belief and emotionality. This ignorance—self-grasping—can be recognized as the cause of all of our suffering, once we are willing to look.

With that recognition, we can easily see the necessity of letting go of both self-cherishing and self-grasping. This is what spiritual practice is all about. A noble practice allows us to act on this recognition and apply the implications of the recognition in our daily lives. With mindfulness, we can begin to discern the quiet, contented ease of self-forgetfulness. We can more quickly recognize the clench of contraction when selfing arises, the heavy mental and emotional and physical weight of defended, strategizing separateness. We can begin to make wiser and more deliberate choices.

The letting go allows us to embody unhindered and spontaneous kindness, both to ourselves and others. This is the noble path and the noble goal of all Dharma, Eastern and Western.

The laying down of self can be mapped. It occurs in stages. These stages could be said to be a map of awakening. Perhaps the simplest way to think of this spiritual transformation, this entrance of attention into awareness beyond self, is to think of it as occurring in three stages: chaos, surrender, and transcendence.

Chaos

For most of us, working through chaos is the arena for our practice. It's Madison Square Garden. We need to keep those bright spotlights shining on our own mind.

Chaos is the experience of our own ignorance, the experience of the charged contents of an unexamined and untrained mind. To the degree that we lead our lives unmindfully, it is our normal state of being. Ordinarily, though, without mindfulness, without investigation, we remain numbed to it, unaware of it.

Chaos is the mind of the self, of selfing, of unconscious habit patterns run wild. The mind of chaos is what is referred to in Buddhism as *dukkha*, or suffering. It is a chronically stressed mind, a mind of taking everything personally, of constant reactivity both gross and subtle. Such a mind is the consequence of delusion, of believing that the self exists in the ways we both conceive of it and perceive it. With such a mind, we're confined to experience within the fractured, chaotic state we create with labeling, separating, judging, resisting, and clinging.

Much of our experience of our lives is the experience of the self's personalized reactivity to whatever is arising. This chronic clinging and defensiveness produces chaos and conflict and stress. Chaos is replete with tension, with ruses, with exhausting attempts to keep the self safe and to choreograph circumstances to optimize illusory promises of happiness or to sidestep all that we do not want.

All of our efforts in this regard are futile. We cannot secure pleasure permanently. We cannot avoid the predictable sufferings.

We cannot will our bodies to stop aging. We cannot will our bodies not to die. We cannot choreograph the universe or "direct the Tao."

We tense and stress ourselves in ways both large and small. We hold ourselves, quite often, in a stance of being "opposed" to reality. We can sometimes even find ourselves feeling that we know better about how the appearance of each moment *should* unfold. Our thoughts, when highlighted, can be quite humbling.

A mind devoid of insight into its own nature is a chaotic mind, a mind of unease.

No matter how savvy and independent and self-controlled we may presume ourselves to be, without mindfulness, chaos is what we discover when we begin to look under the hood. The order we presume with our beliefs is a fragile order, built upon many a mental sleight-of-hand. We've been juggling for a long time.

Think of all we've juggled—occupations, relationships, family, bank accounts, priorities, needs, desires, aversions, hopes, stories, opinions, self-worth and the tightly clinging wish that our own paradigms not be disturbed, that we *can* actually make two and two be five. No wonder we have wrinkles and grey hair.

Often much to our dismay, when we begin to look at our own minds, we find a discordant chorus of reactions to each of the speeding, emotion-packed thoughts that race and rage through it. They chatter over and over in the same patterns, unbidden, unceasingly and exhaustingly, arising in every moment. We find chaos.

ALTHOUGH THERE ARE those whose transformative practices begin in a "pink cloud" experience, most of us find chaos when we first go to sit, to engage in meditation or contemplation or prayer. It can be frightening to see how out of control these minds of ours are. It's sobering to realize how our lack of mindfulness has allowed the very habit patterns that perpetuate our unease to become deeply imprinted. We've stood idly by, unaware, while neural pathways carved deep grooves of selfing that only lead to tension and bewilderment and stress, a contracted state of being in body, mind, and heart.

This realization of how wild and chaotic and harmful are our unmindful thoughts and emotions is known to every practitioner. It is known many times, at increasingly deeper and wider and more subtle levels. It is a rite of passage, a rite replete with insight and humility.

To avoid being disheartened when we first begin a mindfulness or contemplation practice, we should know that this chaos is what we will find. It may seem like, instead of becoming calmer, our minds are becoming crazier. This is not the case. We're just shining a light where no light has shone before. This craziness has been going on for a very long time.

For a brand-new meditator, chaos is the first view of the untamed mind that has always run our experience of existence. It's a little shocking. One friend, turning seventy and turning inward, was sobered to discover what he called "huge chunks of ignorance."

To persevere with our transformative practice, we must have a strong intention to be free of the tyranny of these chaotic thoughts, recognizing the stress and tension that they cause. This intention to be free is amplified when we begin to have some strong intimations or tastes of the peace on the other side, the peace which passeth conceptual understanding.

We can find chaos in our overactive mind, like a car that idles too fast, even when we are experienced meditators. The experience of chaos, the experience of our ordinary minds, is like the crashing of waves in a wild sea sometimes. Mindfulness or contemplative practice can feel like riding a surfboard out through the surges to calmer water. It takes some time to find our balance on the surfboard.

Chaos seems to arise particularly when we have stretched our mindfulness too thin with busy-ness. For most of us, it arises almost instantly with the arising of turbulent circumstances and predictable sufferings.

Without strong mindfulness, chaos can come rushing back, even if we have made some headway in terms of calming it, with any serious shock: surgeries, diagnoses, the loss of our capacity to live independently, or the loss of our loved ones, whether that loss be through their death or their dementia. Without strong mindfulness, we can almost drown in the chaotic turbulence of reactivity.

THE MINDFUL WITNESSING of chaos can highlight our need to cultivate greater equanimity, to keep looking, to keep opening, to ride out beyond the waves that selfing constantly keeps churning. Out beyond the waves, awareness is peaceful enough and still enough, unwavering enough, to observe its own arisings. That stillness is the only platform stable enough to support the presence of clear wisdom. It also is the platform best able to take the most beneficial view of any circumstance and any arising.

Chaos may arise in a longtime meditative practice precisely because we have held the intention for no more dark corners. We *want* to see what craziness remains, so as to work with it and heal it and let it go.

Chaos is an aspect of a transformative experience. It is our experience at the entrance into new and more subtle levels of previously unexamined hindrances. We may experience it initially as bewilderment or confusion as we begin to approach a new substrata of habits, previously hidden from view, but nevertheless affecting our very experience of being.

Each time we sit, we create greater capacity to recognize nonbeneficial habits of mind as they arise. Recognition that the price of ignorant, chaotic thoughts is suffering is the first step toward liberation. We can't transcend what we don't pay attention to. We have to see what binds us in order to loosen the fetters.

The mind of chaos can happen many times, in the course of decades of practice and in the course of a single meditation. In some ways, until a certain point of no return—having passed beyond self, a very high attainment—we're beginners, often lost and battered in chaotic minds for a very long time.

Ordinarily, without the cultivation of mindfulness and wise intention, chaos is our experience when we confront even minor bumps in the road—an hour's wait on the phone with an insurance company, a broken dishwasher, the overturned garbage can after the raccoons had a feast. Our First World problems.

Certainly, for most of us, chaos arises when we face any of the predictable sufferings of a human life. We can drown in deep anguish and overwhelming fear. This is not to say that we will not feel anguish and fear *with* a practice. It is to say that, with a practice, we will have a more stable base from which to observe those incredibly painful and difficult minds, allowing them to pass through with less suffering.

The underlying chaos of ordinary mind is highlighted only through dramatic life passages, when we are forced to become aware of it, or through conscientious attention, when we choose to become aware and stay aware of it. That choice is predicated upon a powerful intention to be free of the obstructions of selfing, to extricate awareness from the stress and unease of chaotic mind.

IN AGING, we may experience the chaos of confronting unexamined beliefs. Perhaps we weren't aware of how much we counted on a desirable appearance or an identity in a function. Perhaps we hadn't realized how attached we have become to respect for our accomplishments and positions, now largely unknown and unnoticed by the younger working crowd that has replaced us in the world. There are some affluent retirement communities where people are referred to as "FIP's"—formerly important people. It's hard to be a "was."

We may experience the chaos of dealing with our reactions to aging bodies gone awry—our own body, our spouse's. One friend noticed that her husband feels "threatened" when she is not well. Another friend noticed his mind's tendency to jump from "ache" to "cancer" with frightening speed.

We may experience chaos in our reactions to the rudeness and indifference with which we, now among the old, may be treated. Or we may experience chaos in our reactions to the kindness with which we, now among the old, may be treated.

Unexpected expenses, illnesses, falls, diminishments push us up against our assumptions about the way things should be, push us face first into the unexamined attachments and aversions that have led us through our years.

Aging offers a thousand opportunities to crash into our own beliefs, a thousand opportunities to crash into the truth of loss and impermanence. A friend, a martial artist at seventy, threw her back out and found the experience humbling. It caused her to recognize that there were more such times to come. Grappling with the question "Who am I without my strength and agility?" she dug more deeply into her own noble path and released some attachment. Her recognition: living is easier to navigate when we become more nonreactive.

The noble path includes every moment.

Staring down chaos, we can recognize that there is no space, no ease, no footing in it. No matter the degree of investment that the self had in attempting to choreograph circumstances, in attempting to sustain what appears to be desirable and keep what appears to be undesirable at bay, it has no traction. The indifferent truth of impermanence will always win. Dying, and to some degree, aging, if we allow it and enable it with mindfulness and intention, are conditions that insist that we stay the course.

For the dying, chaos is the choiceless, scrambling arena in which the end of hope is played out. It is, for those who live with a terminal illness, often a panicked state, revealing how precarious and unstable are the illusions in which we habitually live. There is no refuge in the world of beliefs, in the universe of self. Chaos ensues as we try to resist this truth.

Staying the course—whether through intention, as in a committed spiritual practice, or seeming necessity, as in coming to the time of death—we arrive at the recognition that there is no choice but to cede the victory.

One friend, facing his "only a few months" prognosis, related a dream. His self-image had always involved the need to be "cool," the need to not be "not cool." In the dream, he wandered desperately through a maze-like house, trying to be cool, to appear cool, feel cool, only to come, at the end, to a wall where, cool or not, ego could no longer serve him. He had to lay it down. He discovered, as have so many who have wandered desperately through their own mazes, that the only peace lies in ceding the victory, lies in the laying down of the self.

Aware of the insubstantiality of our beliefs and assumptions and egos, we also become aware that there is a far greater power at play here. That far greater power is the awareness in which this chaos, all of these whirling thoughts and feelings and sensations, is occurring. That far greater power is the endless play of formless presence, the ground of being, unfolding its ephemeral display of forms. And that far greater power, beyond self, is beckoning. For practitioners, our practice of open, mindful looking allows that insight. For the dying, at the end of life, the recognition is stark and starkly given. Surrender becomes the only option.

One day the hero
sits down,
afraid to take
another step,
and the old interior angel
slowly limps in
with her no-nonsense
compassion
and her old secret
and goes ahead.

"Namaste"
you say
and follow.

—DAVID WHYTE

Life, the ground of all being, that old interior angel, has always been beckoning. We've spent so long lost in the form-only world selfing projects that we've missed the sacred formless, aware Presence, calling to us at every moment along the way.

Letting go, we say "Namaste" and follow.

Surrender

Laying down the self, like the hero who is too tired, too weakened, too bored, or too disenchanted with it to keep carrying it around, we cede the victory. Seeing through the self, the hero recognizes it as illusory, mere imputation, and lays it down.

Believing it to be something real and precious, we cling to self. Seeing through the pretense, we drop it; we lose nothing in letting go. It has always been fool's gold. With mindfulness, with steadfast practice, the self is revealed as just an imagined congestion, no refuge at all.

Still, old habits—and surely we must admit, ours are certainly old by now—die hard. As does our belief in the convictions of those habitual thoughts. The truths of suffering, impermanence, and the insubstantial, unfree, constructed nature of the self are the rocks on which the ego begins to break open.

Surrender is a monumental turning point in a life and a known place on any wisdom tradition's map of awakening.

ELISABETH KUBLER-ROSS spoke of the stages of our psychological responses to change. She looked, in particular, at our reactions to change that is perceived as unchosen, our reactions to those circumstances that never would have been chosen. She looked at the psychological responses to the indifferent truth of impermanence.

These psychological stages have become popularized and roll trippingly off the tongue: denial, anger, bargaining, depression, and acceptance. They describe much of our behavior. When we react without mindfulness, these are the mental and emotional places in which we get caught, with all of the physical, mental, and emotional stress that this snagging induces.

These habitual patterns arise with mindfulness also, until a certain point of stability. Although they arise, with mindfulness we have greater insight into them, can recognize them more easily for what they are, and can recognize that we have the capacity to exercise choice in the direction of truth and goodness and beneficial view. Jesus bore witness to that for us. He bargained in the garden before his laying down of the self as an act of piercing wisdom and infinite compassion.

We all get caught—until we don't any longer. Mindfulness and deep intention can grant some skillful means to help loosen us when we do get caught.

Those who observe and companion the dying witness the movement through the psychological stages of coming to terms with the end of one's life. Standing on Kubler-Ross's shoulders, though, there is growing clarity that there is much terrain beyond acceptance.

The terrain, up to acceptance, is the experience of chaos. Denial, anger, bargaining, and depression are part of the dynamic of chaos as it occurs within the conceptual mind of self-cherishing and self-grasping.

ACCEPTANCE IS PSYCHOLOGICAL; it is a stance of the self. The seeming solidity, the congested illusion, of the self remains to endure what must be endured: the dismantling of that self.

The waiting contains dread. At the entry into acceptance, *outer* resistance runs out of gas. Deeper into acceptance, near the Mach band point between acceptance and surrender, resistance continues *inwardly*. The sense of self can feel caught between a chaos that is no longer endurable and a greater power that is frightening in its utter mystery.

We recoil, often, in the midst of a transformative process, from that which we realize to be a far greater power than the illusory ego ever had. The ego comes to be recognized, without a doubt, with no more denial, as an unreliable refuge. It's delusional of us to think of ego as a hiding place. Eventually, one of the predictable sufferings of a human life will kick us out of our contracted, imagined corner, like the friend who ran in his dream only to come up against a wall, the limits of ego in the face of the ground of being.

The bare witnessing of mind's chaos allows the recognition of how far we have lived from the surefooted clarity of truth and from the ease and joy of love. This is so whether the witnessing occurs in the course of dying or in the course of a long-time committed spiritual practice or even during the course of a single meditation.

STRIPPED OF ALL ELSE, the longing for truth, which sees through the illusions of the ego and its fictions, and the longing for love, which yearns to be free of the tension of separateness, assert themselves. As we begin to open our vulnerable hearts to embrace the truth beyond our mind's imaginings, we can begin the U-turn into surrender.

The opening to chaos, to seeing it, confronting it, acknowledging it, and wearying of it, facilitates surrender. The deep and stable witnessing of, rather than the identifying with, the chaos of our own minds reveals the insubstantiality of thoughts and assumptions and passing emotionality. Such witnessing facilitates the surrendering of beliefs, including belief in the confining and bruising dream of self. Beliefs are seen as what they are—passing ephemera, neural firings, no basis for freedom or ease or happiness.

Michael Washburn, a transpersonal thinker, insightfully points out that, in this surrender into awakening, what had been considered to be self-control is seen to be limitation and what had been considered to be independence is seen to be alienation. Who would deliberately, mindfully, choose limitation, choose alienation? We are not here to be small and separate. And, if we have chosen to be so in the past, let's go for broke now.

The fear that got us into the limited existence of "self-control" and the alienation of independence is going to need to come undone. Fear is the ever-present companion of selfing. One goes nowhere without the other.

The strategies of self, arisen in defensiveness, are going to need to come undone if we wish to awaken. Most of us have created so many boundaries between our presumed sense of self and all others and all else. We're constantly scanning for threats, constantly sorting sense data as we imagine it to refer back to self. This reflects our fundamental insecurity and lack of ease. Of course, we're insecure. We've been making it all up.

The strategies of selfing need to be abandoned. Defensiveness not only becomes exhausting but we can begin to recognize it as a futile and draining waste of energy. We have far better things to do with the energy that can be released from defensive habit patterns.

WE CAN WITNESS this movement from chaos to surrender, from the trampling and controlling habits of ego to the laying down of self, in the landmarks of our spiritual journey. We can witness it, as well, in a single session of sitting as we work with self, easing its grasping, stepping out beyond it, letting go. We will witness it, over and over, until surrender is complete, until there is nothing more to let go and we simply let be.

The map of awakening holds true across traditions and holds true whether the movement of deep spiritual growth occurs in a moment or over a decade. Beyond acceptance lies surrender.

Surrender seems frightening to our ordinary, unawakened minds. It is the death of what we've hung on to, the anxious recognition that our ability to control life has always been only imagined. For most of us, it is a fearful entry into the unknown.

Both in dying and in meditative practice, the energy and resources and ploys of the self, previously committed to persevere regardless of the cost, run out of gas. In the case of the dying, they run out through the exhaustion and ravages of terminal illness and the unrelenting assault on the sense of self's assumption of being in control. In an awakening practice, the dynamic of movement from chaos to surrender occurs sometimes out of final and thorough boredom, a world-weariness, with the smallness, the pettiness, and the limitations of the sense of self and its concerns. There is a wise and growing recognition of the sufferings, large and small, that those limitations and concerns hold within them.

Beyond acceptance is a movement into a weariness and a disenchantment with our own contraction. There is a growing compassion for ourselves for having lived in such a cramped, alienated state of unease. There is also a growing compassion for all who've lived around us, whether that be in our home, in the times of our unmindful selfing, or in our world, for any part of our environment we've used selfishly. This increasingly inclusive compassion, this expansion of caring, is one of the flavors of spiritual ripening.

There arises the wish to become harmless. Entering the new terrain of beyond-self, we wave a white flag. For all of the men of our generation who were trained from the playground to be king of the mountain, for all of the women of our generation who were coaxed to grab it all for ourselves because we're worth it, the generosity of harmlessness is a new star on the horizon. It is quickly seen to be a beautiful star, far more steadfast and powerful than the flickering weak light of ego's strategizing.

A shift of the whole being occurs in the recognition of the causes of our own sorrows and stresses. This recognition is surrender. In Buddhism, it's referred to as *renunciation*. The original meaning of the word, as Buddha used it, is "to extinguish." What is to be extinguished is our ignorance, manifesting primarily as belief in a separate self.

We can picture: the tiny ashes of ego—once having assumed itself to be an impressive and eternal firework, now increasingly burned out through the insights of renunciation and surrender—falling into the sea as, one by one, they are extinguished in the water, never to rise again.

There is an entrance into surrender in the conventional sense of the word, the ceding of a victory, the laying down of a self finally stripped of all props and conviction. And there is a growing recognition that the same presence that only a moment before had been so fiercely resisted is that for which we've always longed. The far greater power, at first experienced so fearfully, is realized and experienced as the power of the ground of being, so long obscured by the blindness of selfing. At the moment of surrender, the ground of being, no longer veiled and distorted by a mind trapped in form only, begins to reveal itself as the vast and loving play of form and formlessness, filled with light and ease and vibrancy.

The dynamic is interesting in both dying and in a steady and committed meditative practice. Selfing is resistance. The self does not want to give up its presumed sovereignty. It recoils from transpersonal awareness, sensing, rightly, that that would be the end of "me." And yet, for the small, separate sense of self, a constructed "I" sustained by habit patterns only, there is a dawning realization, in the leap into surrender, that this is the gate into the field of our own deepest longing.

This surrender is paradoxical to conceptual mind. Poetry helps our understanding until we come to know it wordlessly in the intimate depths of our practice.

> That radiance will one day conquer you,
> But only when you have lost everything
> And found that the black of your dissolution
> Is itself nothing but light.
>
> —Jennifer Welwood

For most meditators, this movement into surrender, into beyond-self, is a movement arising from wise effort and wise intention and wise view, gathered and employed many times before transpersonal awareness is stabilized.

Mystery and true refuge both come into play at surrender, at that very edge and with the ambivalence of the experience of that very edge. We may regress in vacillations into false refuge, both wanting and not wanting to move beyond self's paradigm. This mental and emotional vacillation is resolved in transcendence as attention abides in aware presence, at peace in the clarity of the nonconceptual heart, far beyond selfing. Surrender signals that a death has occurred. An ice cube melting in water. Surrender is the death or the cessation of self-grasping and self-cherishing, whether it be momentary or stable. It occurs as a transpersonal movement of mind, a liberation of awareness out of the bounds of self. It is a letting go of selfing. That's the price of admission.

Surrender follows chaos in a moment that feels like a microsecond's breathless pause, a gap. The mind of chaos jumps or is pulled into surrender. This is the pull of beyond-self, once resisted but so quickly seen to be all that was ever yearned for in our deepest prayers of the heart.

There is, in surrender, a feeling of a vortex experience, of being carried away, carried beyond, entering a stream with no other option or desire but to be in its flow. The more experience in it, the more intently we seek to reside in the luminous clarity of pure being.

In a meditative practice, we kind of talk ourselves in, lovingly, gently, tenderly, compassionately speaking to the sense of self that is so afraid it will be left out (it will!) and coaxing it to just let go a little bit more, just step out into beyond-self a little bit further. We coax ourselves into letting go just as we might have nudged our excited but hesitant child through the classroom door on the first day of kindergarten.

Just as in the waves that help birth a baby, each coaxing, based on intention, allows us to open out of self just a tiny bit more.

At the very edge: both death and birth. It is hard to tell them apart in the last moments before surrender enters transcendence.

Transcendence

> When I realized my true being,
> I left behind my human nature to look after itself,
> until its destiny is exhausted.
>
> —Nisargadatta

Surrender is both the cause and effect of the letting go of every fetter. Surrender positions us for transcendence. With a wispier sense of self and growing courage and longing, we remain surrendered. This movement allows us to ripen every positive potentiality, our buddhaseed, our Christ consciousness, in transcendence. Here, as Martin Laird, a contemporary Christian contemplative, puts it, is "not the loss of identity but its flowering."

Transcendence, a state of freedom, follows surrender. It is the experience of awakening, of liberation. This liberation is liberation from attention's entanglement in self, the universe of only form, bound by concept.

Working through chaos is like all of the preparatory work of growing a garden—clearing the soil, adding nutrients, pulling out every opportunistic weed. We do all that we can do. Surrender is simply letting the fruit grow, to be as it will be without any of the ego's machinations. Ego and its strategies are not present in surrender. Surrender allows transcendence: the time of the fruit ripening into maturity, the time of its sharing.

Awareness, in the stage of transcendence, is experienced as increasingly free. At some point of unfolding in the progression of a long and serious and committed practice, awareness is experienced as thoroughly, spontaneously, continuously free, gone beyond form only. In that freedom from the obscurations of selfing, the joy, love, compassion, wisdom, and incomparable sweetness that have always already been here, hidden in plain sight, manifest in their fullness. In transcendence, everything is known as a manifestation of luminous Presence. We recognize our own essential nature as it comes into fruition, ripening every one of the noble qualities to be expressed in our own utterly, endearingly unique way.

THIS PROCESS of chaos, surrender, and transcendence lies in wait for us if we choose to begin or deepen the process of awakening as we age. The period of chaos is tricky but traversing that part of the path leads us to benefits far beyond our imagining. We will confront it anyway if we come to the end of our life without having a spiritual context for our experience of being and a noble, transformative practice.

The potential of this life of ours, however it is for each of us, however circumstances unfold as we age, is far too precious to leave untapped.

Some of the shocks of aging, the awareness of each of our growing list of diminishments, can help us to wake up to the way things are, to wake up out of the dream of self. Our losses and pains and sorrows can be the very things that open us to the grace of living in ever-present awareness, far before the moment of death. We can, as the great Catholic mystic Pierre Teilhard de Chardin suggested, hallow our diminishments. We can, as the nondual teacher Jeff Foster reminds us, allow life to transfigure our losses into an altar.

OPENING THE PRECIOUS PACKAGE

> All we need is to experience what we already possess.
>
> —THOMAS MERTON

EACH OF US has the potential to awaken. This is the immensity of our purpose. This is the value and meaning of this precious human life. Each of us carries the seeds of awakening within this form that formlessness manifests. Ordinarily, most of us are oblivious to the value of the gift we've been given. Many come to the end of their lives never having opened the precious package.

With the intention to use these older years to awaken, the impulse grows to accept the gift, to examine it, to use it.

AN ASPECT OF this gift of a human life is that we all have awareness. Within ever-present awareness there is always contentment and ease. It's naturally simple; it's sane. It simply witnesses. There is nothing not to be contented about. Awareness neither wants nor wants not. It has no investment. There is no suffering in witnessing.

Awareness is peacefully, simply present, always available to abide in. But even after all these years, most of us still remain so unfamiliar with it. We keep it utterly unexamined, an unappreciated, untaken "given."

ORDINARILY, WE MEET every arising experience with a spontaneous feeling of "pleasant" or "unpleasant" or "neither pleasant nor unpleasant." These feeling tones are conditioned; they're impersonal and they arise unbidden. Although they have nothing to do with the self that we imagine, they beckon to the unconscious reactivity of the self.

We get stuck and trapped in unease and misconception when selfing reacts to these feeling tones. In wishing to grasp, to hold on to, what we believe is the cause of pleasant feeling tones, we get stuck in attachment. In wishing to push away, to make disappear, what we believe gives rise to unpleasant feeling tones, we experience the unease of aversion. In reacting indifferently or with bewilderment to what we believe gives rise to feeling tones of neither pleasant nor unpleasant, we separate self from experience and from others, increasing our ignorance and tension. We're like walking Velcro, snags everywhere. Selfing, a reaction mechanism, interferes with the basic sanity that is freely offered us.

As we begin or deepen a committed sitting practice in homage to our growing desire to awaken, we begin to recognize that the experience of awareness is radically different than the experience of being stuck inside of or snagged by the contents of awareness. We begin to become increasingly familiar with sane and simple sentiency and our own obstructions to abiding in that peaceful, agenda-less mind.

Moving through the obstructions, healing and releasing them, is the spiritual path.

To walk this walk of awakening requires open-eyed mindfulness, remembrance of our own longing and insights. To walk this walk also requires a commitment to sit and formally practice. It is in the sitting that we come to perfect the wise and skillful use of the gifts given us with this experience of being.

To have entered a noble path, we have already become familiar with the mental factors of intention and attention, aspects of the precious package. We have developed some facility in using the conjunction of intention and attention as a flashlight, guiding our steps along the path. In a sitting practice, we fine-tune and hone those gifts of intention and attention, developing a more concentrated intensity to their power. Although we may have previously squandered their value many times in our lives, in a committed sitting practice we learn to use them with deliberation in service to our longing.

When we sit, we want to deliberately and wholeheartedly align and conjoin intention (*vitakka,* in Pali) and attention (*vicara,* in Pali). We take the time to do it. We line them up, much as an optometrist aligns and conjoins various lenses to arrive at a corrective prescription aimed at achieving clear physical sight. We align intention and attention to look through them, to see. These "lenses" are unmined treasures. Experiencing what we already possess, as Merton put it, allows our opening into the awakened state.

We have both a microscope to view the infinitesimally small and a telescope to view the unimaginably vast. With intention and attention aligned, we have a lens so finely tuned that it can freeze-frame a nanosecond and zoom into Now.

Intention is not striving or desiring or grasping. We have already tried those strategies in much of our lives and can see where they lead. Intention is simply a setting of course. This gift of the mental factor of intention is best held lightly and used wisely. We will grow in our confidence that wise intention, noble intention, keeps us squarely in the flow of return, resting more and more in the ground of being.

Intention states the direction in which we place our being. It names the destination and the path to the destination. Attention keeps the mind from wandering. Attention follows the compass. Applied attention, unlike our ordinary, untamed minds, is like cohering chaotic light waves to create the power of a laser beam. Applied attention stays on target.

When we practice, we begin with the intention to awaken and the intention to use practice time with skill and wisdom. We place our attention on our chosen object of meditation, whether that be word, sound, breath, a noble quality such as lovingkindness, or the sense of the presence of the sacred.

As we work with concentrating and focusing and stabilizing our attention, we can think of the experience as like that of a tightrope walker. It's the experience of testing the rope, finding stability, walking slowly but with lightness, bringing balance into each next moment.

In the same way, attention finds its balance point with intention's chosen object. Our mental factor of attention holds awareness on the object. Attention may slip, but returning to intention, we once again place attention on the object of meditation as many times as need be. We practice, with the deliberate but light intensity of a tightrope walker, until the attention does not waver at all from its object.

CONTENTED EASE (*piti*, in Pali) will arise as attention remains more stable. All hindrances to ease—the retinues of ego, such as attachment, aversion, agitation, torpor, and doubt—begin to melt away in the intensity of the continued application of attention. We don't try to generate ease—the very trying blocks it; we simply notice its arising.

In that ease, we can begin to relax these tired, aching bodies, still carrying the consequences of decades of stress and unease. We can lean back into the arising ease as if it were a hammock. We can relax thoroughly in it, as if we were floating on our back in a mirror-like lake, motionless except perhaps for the tiny, silky movement of a finger through the water every once in a while.

Ease relaxes the body and the mind. It allows the body a vacation from tension and contraction and allows the mind a vacation from the constant conceptualizing that always scans the horizon, like a giant radio telescope searching for salient frequencies. The ease of doing just one simple thing with total attention is refreshing and exhilarating. It is the ease of being, the ease of freedom from our habitual multitasking.

Ease brings about the stilling of our constantly churning mental images and our habituated patterns. There is little ego to be found in such deep ease. Resistance begins to release and we begin to deeply relax, to surrender into undefended peace.

JOY (*sukha*, in Pali) arises out of such deep ease. Joy arises with surrender, with the sane and natural trust that engendered surrender. Again, we don't need to generate it. We simply note the joy naturally arising and experience it mindfully. It is the taste of increasingly bare, increasingly subtle awareness. Hildegard of Bingen, the medieval mystic, advised "be not lax in celebrating." Buddha suggested that we allow our bodies to be suffused with joy. We let joy play upon us, like a lover. Eventually, all resistance, the very nature of selfing, melts in the surrendering.

Some dusting of self can still remain for a while at this level of subtlety, for practitioners within any tradition. We want to watch here for whatever wisps of ego follow the urge to grasp at or try to own the joy. There is no need to grasp at it. It is always present, always within the airy, easy spaciousness of now. It is not possible to own it.

We've concocted a thousand scenarios over all these decades of ours in the belief that they would lead us to joy. We have believed for so long that the cause of joy was outside of us. Other-worldly joy, joy spontaneously generated with the wise use of our gifts, has nothing to do with anything that appears to be external. It skips the middle man completely.

In a sitting practice, keeping the minds of intention and attention and ease aligned, joy can arise to the point where it cascades through the body, and we feel as if we couldn't possibly contain any more joy. With continued practice, though, our experience of being expands into a vastness that can contain everything. There is a sense of no boundaries whatsoever to containing it all.

Joy increases the experience of stability within intention and attention and ease. Having found what we have always been looking for, the mind has no need to wander. If we do waver in our focus, we go back to the place where we lost it. Perhaps we can move back to joy by going back to ease. Other times, we may have to go all the way back to intention and strengthen it, enliven it again. All of this we do lightly, without striving, without desiring, simply working with wise operating instructions.

In this space of joy dawns wonder and awe, the cooling and absorbing alertness of curiosity. Curiosity (*ekagattta*, in Pali) is naked inquiry, single-pointedly focused on each moment's arising of the object of attention. This absorption enfolds many layers of subtlety. It is engendered naturally through the stable alignment of the first four minds: intention, attention, ease, and joy. It arises naturally when the self is no longer so congestedly present, when selfing's fears of seeing what lies beyond the horizons of its own paradigm are no longer so obstructive.

Curiosity is a mind controlling nothing. It is a mind without prejudice or expectation, a mind undefended by conception and agendas. It becomes absorbed in and fascinated by the ever-novel and endless display of the ground of being.

Deeply curious, we enter absorption, concentrating vastness, deepening the awe and wonder. The experience here is so absorbing that, merging with the point of concentration, awareness rushes into another world, mushrooming out into vastness, free of all self-reference and any localized sense. This is a domain of subtle lucidity and radiance beyond self. Vastness is so increased that the self doesn't even appear as a distant horizon. Awareness floats, a sea of tranquility. Radiant and alive and filled with every quality of grace.

Awed and innocent curiosity deepen in this meditative state. We embody increased wisdom and compassion as we arise from meditation—they are the fruits of the insights of clear seeing.

INTENTION. ATTENTION. EASE. JOY. CURIOSITY. We line them up as a child would line up presents. These are *our* presents. When we finally begin using these gifts wisely, we, old as we are, end up with the fresh new immaculate wonder of a child.

THE SPECIAL CONDITIONS

I do not understand
the mystery of grace—
only that it meets us where we are
and does not leave us
where it found us.

—Anne Lamott

GATHERING THE SPECIAL CONDITIONS

> Beloved,
> there is much we can do
> to open ourselves to receiving His favors.
>
> —Saint Teresa of Avila

Conditions without number come into confluence and engender all arisings. Conditions without number, impossible to count or even to imagine, give rise to the birth of a star in the heavens, a tsunami, a baby, a psychopath, a watermelon, a rain shower.

The endless dance of awareness and appearances unceasingly gives rise to moments of mind that abide and then dissolve.

Each of us has a different, a unique, experience of the arising appearances of the world in which we live, determined by the habits of our own mind and the intentions that we hold. Our desires, our tendencies, and our habitual patterns determine the way that we conceive of and perceive and experience these endlessly arising appearances. These desires and tendencies and habits are karma:

patterned movements of mind with agendas, including agendas that reside in unconsciousness.

Everything we see is a reflection of our own mind, with its deep karmic imprints. Everything. Without mindfulness, the direction of these movements of mind is random in terms of benefit, unguided in terms of wisdom.

Without mindfulness, the arising appearances shaped by our karma are often chaotic and unsettling. The arisings continue in reverberating trajectories, ongoing variations on a theme. Our habituations perpetuate the same old patterns—angry, unappreciated, right, restless, less than, confused, jealous, threatened, entitled, anxious. They arise from lack of mindfulness and lack of wise intention, over and over, in endless permutations.

As Shakespeare described it: "It is a tale told by an idiot, full of sound and fury, signifying nothing." And, until we deliberately enter a path of growing mindfulness, so it continues.

WITH MINDFULNESS, WE add creativity. Creativity doesn't even arise in a mind closed in on itself, in a mind that is exclusively self-referential, that tiptoes around life, afraid of rocking its own paradigm's boat. Mindfulness allows creativity. It allows a moment to be approached freshly. Mindfulness adds the spaciousness of a tiny bit of dis-identification. This spaciousness allows formless awareness to work its magic on the fulcrum of our wise intention.

Mindful awareness recognizes that there are options. Every nanosecond's experience can be guided with intention, aligned with intention, taking the present trajectory of arisings and setting it on a new path.

When we decide that we want to cook, we need to actually turn on the stove. In the same way, when we decide that we wish to investigate the vast potentialities of our birthright as human beings and ripen them, we need to apply this intention, take the actions of commitment, and see the transformative process through to maturity. We need to apply mindfulness and intention, the creative aspects, the transformative aspects, to each new moment's appearance that arises prefigured by our habitual karmic habits.

We want to harness our energy. We want to harness and ingather and cohere our energy in alignment with our intention. This is making skillful use of the faculties available in each of us.

Unharnessed energy is wasted. It's squandered, as have been so many of the tens of thousands of unmindful moments in our lives. Unharnessed energy can be destructive. Think of a tornado or a flood. Think of electricity sparking out of a broken, downed wire. Unharnessed energy can harm others. Is there any part of our finer selves, much less our essential being, that would deliberately wish to harm another? Think of all the many times we've said something in anger, wishing even as the words are coming out of our mouths that we could reel them back in. Unharnessed energy can harm us. It is often the cause of our own suffering—our own past suffering, our own present suffering, and our future suffering.

To stay mindful, we need to create some special conditions in our lives. We need to assemble the special conditions that can usher in our awakening. What a waste it would be to enter the time of dying, now looming larger on our horizons like a ship sailing into the harbor, with the same old petty and weary thoughts and reactions running through our mind.

We do not want our lives to signify nothing. This would be the most profound and ungrateful ignorance: to remain childish in an aging vessel.

All creation will delight as we allow our own liberation. The ground of being embraces us in welcome, each and every one of us, as we progressively emerge from self to soul to spirit. Life's longing for itself is a path of grace.

THESE DECADES OF our lives, our "senior citizen" years, can call forth urges and longings, deeper than those of the ego, larger and more spacious than those of the self. The thoughtfulness these urges and longings provoke may have arisen before, in younger years, in quiet moments under the stars or rocking our baby or weeding around a carrot row. This thoughtfulness has often been pushed to the background by many of us in the decades of busy-ness.

For many of us as we age, this thoughtfulness begins to emerge into the foreground. Carl Jung, the eminent Swiss explorer of the psyche, said he never met a person in the latter part of his or her life who came to him for counsel who was not seeking counsel about things spiritual in nature.

Aging most often brings with it a greater degree of quiet than we've experienced before as well: the luxury of some time and space. It gives us the leisure to go around and take inventory, to look and see what longings and intimations we've stashed away on the shelf and forgotten for years.

With each passing week, the likelihood increases that we will confront circumstances that jar our complacency. We're walking time bombs, even with a clean bill of health. Any unsettling circumstance can stir us to dust off, examine, and contemplate those deeper urges, yearnings, and intuitions.

Aging can bring with it a sense of time running out, the recognition that this personal life is coming to an end. This is the catalyst of urgency. The call of those deeper urges and longings can be heard now, as the outer, worldly din lessens. Our alertness grows with the sense of urgency.

We can begin to experience our separate sense of self, the illusion so carefully constructed, as a tense, contracted prison of separation, blocking connection. We can begin to experience all of the unmindful, habituated patterns upon which we impute our sense of self as our own barrier to the joy of simply being. The walls of selfing block both inflow and outflow. They keep us small and trapped.

It is helpful to keep inquiring, to keep asking the kind of piercing questions whose answers are not easy to ignore. How many barriers have we put up to love and to openness? What has that cost us? How have we hidden the very vulnerability that allows connection? How many times have the same triggers evoked the same knee-jerk reactions? How sobering it can be to see ourselves as automatons, believing we have freedom and seeing how enslaved we are in our own habits.

Chogyam Trungpa, a Tibetan teacher of great wisdom, urged us to look at how petty and confined we keep ourselves, how enslaved. A great deal of unease arises in the experience of a small and limited life, in believing ourselves to be unchangeably, inescapably, smaller and more limited than we are in essence, in truth.

Mindfulness allows us to experience the contracted state in which we've held our awareness and experience of being. Applying mindfulness to an ordinary moment is a bit like sliding slowly into a bubbling, hot mineral pool and, upon relaxing, recognizing in what tension we've held ourselves.

As we age, we may become increasingly aware of a sustained insistence, of a deeper need for more freedom in our being. How long can we stand it in these knotted layers of tension and confusion, hoping to please or achieve or meet expectations? One older friend, contemplating what she wished to do with her last years, shared that she was sick of having judgment control virtually every aspect of her experience and her expression and intended to change that. Another friend, sick of being controlled by politeness. Another, so tired of feeling the need to prove himself.

At this point in our lives, many of us want the keys to freedom.

> The small man
> builds cages for everyone he knows,
> while the sage,
> . . . .
> keeps dropping keys all night long
> for the beautiful rowdy prisoners.
> —HAFIZ

THE DESIRE to end the reactivity, that ever-jerking knee, and the desire for more stable peace of mind, liberated from self and circumstance, can lead us to begin to develop a new way of living, a new and freer way of being in the world, a way that will sustain us in whatever circumstances might arise as we age.

We can initiate this liberation from limitation and unease, liberation from self, the very source of unease, with a stable and committed spiritual practice, sustained by creating wise and skillful circumstances for ourselves. We want to deliberately create in our lives the special conditions that nurture awakening from the dream of self, the confined known world of form only.

C. S. Lewis had insight into the special conditions that either nurture awakening or foster remaining asleep. To awaken, we need to sit up straight. In *The Screwtape Letters*, a senior demon suggests to a devil-in-training that human beings should be urged to remain slouching.

Throughout the ages, humanity's explorers and lovers of spirit, those who have taken the path before us, have learned that special conditions are needed to move awareness beyond identification with the personal, separate sense of self. Skillful means, authentic and powerful practices designed to achieve such a goal, have been developed.

These authentic skillful means—the deep inner practices of Christianity, Judaism, Islam, Taoism, Hinduism, and Buddhism, for example—form our meditative, contemplative spiritual heritage. We have other heritages, necessary for the survival of life-in-form, in fire and water and earth and air. This contemplative heritage, though, is the richest heritage on the planet. It can open the door to formless awareness, beyond self.

OUR INTENTION to attain liberation from self needs to outwit our attachment to and identification with self. Special conditions are circumstances we provide for the self until we can be free of the self. Moral discipline is the place to begin if we wish to outwit selfing. Many traditions offer guidelines for moral discipline.

Although our inner teenager may rebel against the notion of moral discipline, it is wise view, mature view, to hold the practice of moral discipline in our mind as a practice that is for our own benefit. We practice moral discipline because we choose to. Our moral discipline can benefit others, certainly, but we are not doing it to please or appease them. We are doing it to strengthen the integrity of our intention, just as we would exercise to strengthen our muscles and heart. We do it to decrease distractions and lessen the tight grip ignorance has had on our attention.

The adoption of a practice of moral discipline with the intention of one day utterly embodying the practice is a wise act.

> after weeks of watching the roof leak
> I fixed it tonight
> by moving a single board
>
> —GARY SNYDER

Moral discipline provides a protection circle for our fledging practice. It is good to remember, even for those who have practiced for a long time, that our practice is fledgling, until we are soaring and free.

The discipline protects us. It keeps us from feeding the old habit patterns that have never led to happiness, that have always led to tension and unease. Gurdjieff, the Russian mystic, once defined sin as that which we do to keep ourselves asleep after we've already decided to awaken. A practice of moral discipline keeps us from such "occasions of sin."

The discipline grows confidence. It highlights the urges of the self as they crash into the barrier of the moral discipline. This gives us the opportunity to practice maintaining a higher level of intention than the energy level of those urges. This keeps us from getting carried out to sea in the powerful undertows of urge and story and reaction and self.

Moral discipline clears distractions. It creates enough space so that we can stay in remembrance. It keeps us from slouching.

IN TIBETAN BUDDHISM, moral discipline is practiced by abandoning, with intention and over time, what are called the ten nonvirtuous actions. The name derives from the view that virtuous actions are those that lead to the happiness of awakening, while nonvirtuous actions are those that keep us trapped in the suffering that ignorance creates.

In this yoke, or union, with moral discipline, we avoid killing, stealing, sexual misconduct, lying, divisive speech, hurtful speech, idle chatter, covetousness, malice, and wrong view. Refraining from engaging in these actions, we extinguish the tendencies that give rise to them and eliminate the suffering they would cause.

The nonvirtuous actions feed the very self from which we wish to liberate our attachment. They deepen our mistaken sense of existing in the separate, unconditioned way in which we believe our selves to exist.

Moral discipline is the intention to one day be able to keep the commitment to abstain from these unwise actions, such roadblocks to awakening.

THE THREE NONVIRTUOUS actions of body (killing, stealing, sexual misconduct) enmesh us in ignorance, ensnare us in harm and suffering. We can work to abandon them and to open our minds into a wiser view. As our view embraces more wisdom, the habituated impulses to engage in nonvirtuous actions will begin to atrophy. Wise view will naturally give rise to actions that not only emerge from a more awakened understanding but will also lead us to further awakening. When we change our view, we change our experience of being.

Killing keeps us separate from the hallowed flow of life. Instead, we can practice with a wondrous respect for life—deep appreciation for the sentiency of all its dazzling forms, each with the same wish to be happy and to be free from suffering. Every form that we encounter is not other than the sacred formless, a manifestation of the holy. When we engage in such a remembrance practice, even before we have realized the truth of the view, we realize the majesty of being and begin to live in a new way, deeply and more joyfully in the divine flow, interconnected, interdependent.

Stealing, taking anything that isn't freely given, keeps us separate from trust. We deny ourselves the opportunity to relax in deep faith, in the confidence that comes from knowing our own essential nature as safe, as trustworthy. We mire ourselves more deeply in separation and defendedness, hiding more deeply in greedy clinging and selfing. We can cultivate the wise and compassionate practice of generosity, clinging to nothing, happy to share. We were taught this in kindergarten. If we haven't yet embodied the lesson, now would be a good time to do so. There is a rush of joy and freedom when we stop clinging and wanting.

Sexual misconduct keeps us separate from integrity and from each other. We become more bound in isolation and alienation. We can, instead, practice deep respect for personhood, reining in whatever tendencies remain in us to objectify others, to use others for self-serving goals, sexual or otherwise. We can practice living in what Buddha called "the bliss of blamelessness."

THE FOUR NONVIRTUOUS ACTIONS of speech (lying, divisive speech, hurtful speech, and idle chatter) perpetuate ignorance. They cosign the story lines of the self.

Lying keeps us separate from the truth. We can practice letting go of all of our fictions, including the fiction of a separate self. We can practice the love of truth and a pervading, mindful inquiry that allows our ongoing insight into it.

Divisive speech renders us separate from the wonder and the refuge of interbeing. We make ourselves smaller with "enemy camps" and exclusivity, with the need to be "right" or "better." We head in the wrong direction, back to sleep, when we do so. A far more liberating way of being in our daily lives is to live in deep appreciation for the communal ground of being from which we all arise. We can live humbly in the recognition that our ordinary minds understand so little, that our mental chatter is permeated with ignorance and the needs of selfing. Divisiveness harms; inclusiveness will not.

Hurtful speech keeps us separate from compassion, pushes attention right out of the flow of awakening. There is enough suffering in the world—no need to add to its sum total. Only ignorance would add more. We can practice living in the compassionate recognition that being a person is difficult, that every being's wish to be free from suffering is identical to our own wish, and that pain is pain regardless of who appears to be experiencing it. Rather than engaging in hurtful speech, we can practice speaking from the mind of lovingkindness, a mind of cherishing others.

Idle chatter and gossip carry us, like a rip tide, out of wise intention and wise effort. We mire ourselves more deeply in our stories and unexamined assumptions, increasing our entanglement in the inessential and the mistaken. When we engage in idle chatter, we allow unmindfulness to hold sway, keeping us in the periphery of being, further away from all that is good and true and beautiful. We can practice wise speech, speech in service to awakening.

THE THREE NONVIRTUOUS actions of mind (covetousness, malice, and wrong view) obstruct liberation and awakening. They keep us trapped in stress and smallness, so much less than the precious gift this life offers us.

Covetousness keeps us separate from the very contentment we seek. When we covet, we knock ourselves right out of the peace of equanimity and the deep joy of gratitude. We can, instead, deliberately engage in the practice of appreciation. Appreciation neutralizes attachment. In the mind of appreciation, we are grateful for all of the beauty and goodness that arises in our minds, grateful for the grace of our own noble intention, grateful for the love in which we always live. From that stance of already-fulfilled appreciation, we can rejoice in each other's happiness. There is so little genuine happiness. Rejoicing in another's happiness, we enter joy.

Malice keeps us separate from the goodness of our own essential nature. We can practice taking the perspective of another—a certain sign of awakening—and act within the simple rule of doing unto others as we would have them do unto us. There is a reason every wisdom tradition teaches love. It is the express train to awakening. In love—a heart space, a nonconceptual experience of being—there is, as one friend put it, "the spinning collapse of the space between us." The powerful wish to be harmless arises.

Holding wrong views keeps us separate from wisdom, from clear seeing. It keeps us trapped in the mistaken assumptions of the conceptual mind, the home of selfing, far from the clarity of awareness. We circle endlessly in ignorance, suffering within that circling, when we cling to our conviction that the raw sense data we process and the conclusions our conceptual minds come to as a consequence are the final statements on the way things exist. We can engage, in each moment, in the practice of naked inquiry—dropping preconceptions, asking "what is this?" of each arising. We hone this capacity to look, to inquire, in formal practice and can engage it throughout the day. When we stop ignoring what is really so in each new moment, we are no longer so bound in ignorance.

IF WE'RE USING this time of aging to find release from the stresses of our own mind's creation, this skillful means of adopting moral discipline creates the conditions to see ourselves more clearly. We can heal what needs to be healed and begin to transform our self-cherishing habits, as well as that most deeply rutted of habits: grasping to a self.

Other traditions offer guidelines for moral discipline, certainly. Such wisdom did not just arise in Buddhism. We have quite a few laundry lists to choose from, the adoption of any of which will guide our way home: the Ten Commandments, the Six Perfections, the Five Precepts, the Seven Deadly Sins, the Eightfold Path.

Perhaps the simplest guideline, as simply elegant as Einstein's $E=mc^2$, is Jesus's suggestion that we love one another.

Adopting a moral discipline clears the space of our awareness, of our daily lives, of distractions. One couple found that they tended to judge others in the casual conversations they had between themselves. They made a commitment to stop. They found that the adoption of just this one practice of abstaining from judging others allowed them entry into examining their behavior, and transforming their behavior, in the light of all of the other aspects of practicing moral discipline.

Moral discipline opens things up. It empties out a lot of behaviors and thoughts that are not only meaningless but harmful to our intention to awaken from the dream of self.

This newly opened space allows us to invite in, to deliberately create in our lives, the special conditions that nurture our awakening. Special conditions, again, are actions we can impose upon the self, things that we can do with the self until we can be free of the self. Any gathering of spiritual practitioners from every tradition assembles a body of wisdom regarding how to till the soil. Remarkably similar conditions are engaged in all wisdom lineages.

THE SPECIAL CONDITIONS catalyzing transformation are also the same conditions that arise at the time of death, a moment of profound spiritual transformation in the life of any and every human being. These special conditions that arise at the end of life facilitate the surrender into the grace in dying, the radical liberation of awareness into grace.

We can observe them arising as we sit with someone who is dying. What we will observe, if we have the privilege to be present with someone at the end of his or her life, are the following special conditions: opening to mortality, withdrawal, silence, solitude, forgiveness, humility, the practice of presence, commitment, life review and resolution, opening the heart, and opening the mind. Those of us who are still living can take powerful lessons from the dying.

Each of these special conditions is a powerful catalyst for transformation. They release us from grasping to self. Working skillfully, we can introduce and make use of these conditions in the midst of life, in these very chapters of being old. Just as these special conditions facilitate the grace in dying, they can lead us directly into the grace in living.

- Opening to our own mortality is a liberation from pettiness and the smallness of selfing. It allows a release from the inessential.
- Withdrawal allows freedom from the blind habits upon which we impute our sense of self.
- Silence engenders a liberation from illusions and from the internal monologue that so convinces us of the reality of self.
- Solitude brings us to a stable platform from which we can liberate attention from attachments.
- Forgiveness liberates us from anger and from judgment. It allows a release of attention from the mental affliction of aversion.
- Humility unfolds into freedom from pride and the illusions of perfectionism. It is a liberation into ordinariness.
- The practice of moment-by-moment presence, breath-by-breath awareness, emancipates attention from frivolity, from all that is meaningless, from all of the ways in which we squander this precious human life.
- Commitment entails "taking the one seat." It is a way of describing the conditions of a committed, earnest practice and the choiceless conditions of dying. It liberates us from wavering, from wandering in our attention and intention. Taking the one seat eliminates the escape routes.
- The work of life review, leading to life resolution, releases us from our story. It is the work of self-inquiry. It engenders a liberation into the freedom of presence—into experiential attention, free from narrative.
- Opening the heart liberates us from the limitations of fear. It is here that we enter into awareness beyond self. It brings us to

communion, directly into love. It is one of the great tasks and the great joys of a human experience.

- Opening the mind is to make space in the mind. It emancipates our attention from the distractions of assumptions and reactions. It also frees us from our beliefs, from all that we think we know. It allows entrance into the wonder of the great mystery and the wisdom clarity of direct knowing. It, also, is an essential task of awakening.

We will know and experience these special conditions that nurture spiritual transformation when it is our time to begin to die. It is kind and it is wise to gather these special conditions, to put them in place in our lives, long before our last breath. They facilitate the surrender of self-cherishing and self-grasping.

Gathering the special conditions of transformation increases the possibility of release, free from attachment to self, into the present moment. Shantideva, a realized Tibetan monk from centuries ago, calls this "nonreferential ease." No more of the fiction that is filled at every turn with self-reference. No more of the tension and the stress and the posturing and the quiet despair of self-reference.

We now, in these last chapters of our life, have the time and the humility and the life wisdom to appreciate the preciousness of this fleeting experience. Stepping over the threshold of attachment to self, stepping out of self and beyond self, our awareness is filled with grace, is graced with the true and the good and the beautiful, all always already ever-present.

The special conditions of transformation are skillful means by which we can organize our life around our intention. We act with both wisdom and self-compassion when we choose to use these later years as a retreat and dedicate them as such. We don't need to go to a cave or a monastery. We don't need an isolated hut in the woods. We just need a commitment to awaken. We need the wise gathering of the special conditions that will facilitate awakening. We need earnest, steadfast practice.

The retreat doesn't need a place. It needs an intention. It is a mental space. Intention is our enclosure. It is an enclosure that expands to include everything.

We can incorporate all of the special conditions of transformation deliberately and mindfully, using them as retreat boundaries. Retreat boundaries are a bit like moral discipline in that they protect us from our own selfing. The retreat boundaries we choose for the rest of our lives are entirely up to us. We choose which actions of body, speech, and mind we will engage in and which we will not.

These retreat boundaries may tighten at times, open at times. Visits with friends and family, travel, or the generous actions of social involvement may, at times, be exactly where we need to be. At other times, more solitude may be appropriate.

The cycle of solitude and engagement is like breathing; it always moves between "in" and "out." As we begin to become more adept in our practice and more earnest in our intention, our wisdom will grow. We will increasingly be able to discriminate between genuine spiritual aspiration, the wish to free awareness from attachment to self, and the ego's urges. We will be able to begin to trust ourselves a bit more.

The important thing is that these decisions be made mindfully. The question to ask is simple: Does seclusion from the world at this moment, or engagement in the world at this time, support the relaxation of the contraction of self? Or does it increase selfing's ignorant grasp? If we want to designate these last chapters as awakening chapters, we need to hold all of the moments in them under the umbrella of awakening, in the light of mindful awareness.

OPENING TO OUR OWN MORTALITY

MEDITATION ON DEATH

The longer we are together
the larger death grows around us.
How many we know by now
who are dead! We, who were young,
now count the cost of having been . . .
Our hair turns white with our ripening
as though to fly away in some
coming wind, bearing the seed
of what we know. It was bitter to learn
that we come to death as we come
to love, bitter to face
the just and solving welcome
that death prepares. But that is bitter
only to the ignorant, who pray
it will not happen. Having come
the bitter way to better prayer, we have
the sweetness of ripening.

—Wendell Berry

We cannot speak about aging and awakening without speaking about death and dying; it certainly seems to come up at every turn. We need to confront our mortality.

Although there probably occurred deep transformation, deep release, for those Inuit elders who, on their tiny islands of ice, floated away from their villages and their loved ones, this isn't a call to "hop on an iceberg." Perhaps we can think of it as a call to the iceberg experience.

Meditating on death opens us up deeply to the precious gift of this life and the boundless gift we can make of it. It begs us to look at what remains frivolous in our lives, what remains careless. Most of us have lived so many decades on the surface of being, whistling around the outskirts of awareness.

We rarely pause to question, to look. Where have I not forgiven? Where have I not apologized? Who have I not loved well? Who have I not thanked? Where do I still cling? What fears do I still harbor? Such deeply and thoroughly honest contemplation allows us to change what can be changed and die with less regret.

Meditating on death is one of the special conditions that facilitates spiritual transformation, illumination. Wisdom traditions have employed it as skillful means for millennia. It is, at the end of life, one of the most powerful of the special conditions that facilitates the grace in dying. When we are deeply aware of our own impermanence, every fleeting moment is recognized as precious. Our desire to be present in each moment amplifies. Contemplating the fact that we truly do not know if we will still be alive in this human body with the next breath, we can witness a stunning decrease in our attachment to and interest in anything but now. Presence begins to blossom.

Meditating on death instantly calls us to question on the deepest of levels. What am I doing? What do I want? What does this all mean? What is it all about? What is spirit? What is self? Who or what is the "I" that is asking the questions? Our desire to explore, to inquire, to see, intensifies in urgency.

We have no idea how much time each of us has left to clearly see—which is to say, awaken.

Contemplating our own mortality, taking in the fact of our mortality, our precariously impermanent existence, can call us to complete and thorough accountability. It can call us to instant reordering, a rearranging of our priorities and our intentions. A deep opening to our own mortality brings us to our knees and down to the nitty-gritty. It blocks off all of our habitual detours into denial. It forces us to face the way we've lived our lives, the choices we've made, the polestars we've chosen.

Contemplating our own mortality can spur a sense of urgency. The urgency is not to panic and try harder, squinching up and exerting and striving. The urgency is to become more earnest, more sincere, more aligned in our spiritual intention. The urgency reminds us to become less frivolous, to remain mindful of our deepest intention, to not allow our experience of being to sink so carelessly into mindlessness.

The Pali language has a word, *samvega*, that refers to the urgent need to practice, to engage in awakening practices. It denotes a healthy desire that can arise out of a heightened sense of our own mortality, our own ephemeral impermanence.

Meditating on death allows us to take the conceptual understandings that we will die and that the time of our death is uncertain to the level of our heart. That distance—from head to heart—is a long journey with many roadblocks, many obstacles, many bumps in the road.

Meditating on our own death allows us to open to a truth. Opening to the truth, we marinate in it. We allow understanding and insight into that truth to percolate and permeate our being, pruning the old neural connections of mindless habits, and allowing new neural pathways, new and more beneficial habits of mind, to come into operation and flourish.

Contemplating our own mortality can bring concept into direct experience. It is a journey from nodding intellectual understanding of the concept of impermanence to the experience of it as a moment-by-moment reality. To take in that we will die and that it is uncertain when—that it could be anytime, even this moment—at the level of our heart is an understanding of the whole being that can actually affect and transform us.

If we keep the fact of our mortality at the level of conception, in our head, it remains as just another piece of information, like the number of calories in a dish of ice cream or how to plant a tomato seedling. When we take it into our heart, the truth of the recognition knocks every cell in our being with the shock. We get it. It is so.

We cut off a lot of recognition at the level of our neck. We block the very truth that will set us free.

THERE IS NOTHING that can keep us from death. No pleading, begging, or bribing. The world offers no shelter from death. There is no one who can protect us.

When we die, the world our mind experienced will be swept away. It does not endure, just as this passing phenomenon we call "me" does not endure. When we die, all of our thoughts and concerns, all of our prides and attachments—our universe—will cease.

Our eyeglasses will be useless to anyone else. The objects we so loved will be priced for a tag sale, a penny on the dollar. Someone else will access our accounts and sell the car we dreamed of for so long. Someone will cut down the roses we planted so many years ago and tended so carefully. Someone will paint the house a different color or maybe even raze it.

Everything that we are concerned about in this very moment will not matter at all: bills, quarrels, sensed inadequacies, the sale at the mall, fears, vanities, hopes for the stock market, what to have for dinner. They will not matter at all.

Although we have been a slave to craving and aversion for all of these decades, when we die we leave every illusory object of craving and aversion behind.

We leave self behind. It was always a fiction—allowing functionality certainly, but a fiction nonetheless. We mistakenly took everything personally. Death is a letting-go of this sense of personalization, of self-reference. Our liberation occurs in a larger perspective.

We've lived in the unease and the difficulty of taking everything personally. We have spent a long time fretting over, defending, preening, despairing over a sense of self that has always been both a deeply invested concept and an illusion.

> You have enclosed yourself in time and space,
> squeezed yourself into the span of a lifetime
> and the volume of a body. . . .
> You cannot be rid of problems
> without abandoning illusions.
>
> —NISARGADATTA

Let's change this before we die.

IT IS THE NATURE of selfing to find life problematic. With that view, a new problem, like another wave on the ocean, will always arise. We're now old enough to recognize that it is not relief from problems that we want so much; we have a growing sense that relief is only a temporary respite. It does not last. We want the experience of unshakeable peace in the face of any arising, every new wave. We want the grace that only lies in awareness freed from self-reference, self-grasping, self-cherishing. Such awareness is freed from reactively personalizing each wave.

Ken McLeod, an American Dharma teacher, has said that at every stage of practice, there is a price to be paid for increased clarity and greater freedom. The price, he says, is the loss of another illusion. It seems helpful to think of our illusions as tokens for the ride. We grieve our way to awakening, paying our way with the release of all of our cherished and convincing fictions. We drop them one by one, the footsteps of our path.

Jesus bore witness to the truth of awakening from the dream of self. In Gethsemane, he shared the human being that he was—aware of his own singularity, aware of self. Even with the depth of his realizations and the magnitude of his love, he experienced the angst of his own impending death.

Jesus prayed, in Gethsemane, for his passageway through the chaotic minds of clinging and reluctance. Surrendering, arms wide open on the cross, he entered the dying process and emerged as Christ consciousness, transcendent.

There is profound beauty in the view, the example, of Jesus's offering, his surrender.

THE IMMENSITY of his act is worthy of deep reverence and respect, even awe. It doesn't, though, need to cause us to back away from the spiritual journey as if the journey and the arrival hidden within it are beyond our capacity. His was an encouraging act, not a discouraging one. It would be a mistake to contemplate the meaning of the act and arrive at the conclusion that the journey is something for others who are more "worthy" or "braver" or more "evolved."

We don't need to climb a cross to attain this degree of liberation or spend thirty years in a cave. Nothing so dramatic. Wisdom traditions abound with such inspirations and examples because it takes a lot to inspire us. It takes a very loud wake-up call to rouse us from sleep.

We're all ordinary beings, and it is completely possible, with intention and effort, to free ourselves from the confines of selfing in our ordinary lives. It is possible to do this in a completely, beautifully, ordinary way. We can do it in our house, on our street, within our family. Still voting, still cooking, still waving to the neighbors, shouting "fore" before we swing, and stopping at the stop sign.

One of the biggest spurs for our journey can come with deep and regular contemplation of our own mortality as a focal point, as an ever-present truth to hold in awareness. It, more than just about any other contemplation, forces us to ask questions at a level of depth from which we may never have inquired before. Where am I most deeply attached? Where am I most deeply anxious? What will be lost? What is it that dies?

A friend, at seventy, accepted that her last lessons might well come through her body. Having given up all else, she said, that will be the learning lab. Perhaps that's true for all of us. There are questions to explore. Am I this flesh I sense and perceive? What is the nature of my relationship with this body I call "me" or "mine"? How does mind impute "I" on fleeting sensations?

We can practice meditating as though this body were dying, a profound and skillful way to practice. We can come to intimately know the unfolding stages of chaos, surrender, and transcendence in a frequent contemplation of our own mortality. Saint Augustine recognized this when he counseled all who sought his heart-felt advice to "die daily."

When we sit to meditate on mortality, we can think that this may be the last time we may ever be able to do this. The power of that thought lies in the fact that the statement holds truth. We can sit to meditate with the intention to imitate death. We can sit to meditate with the intention to let it all go, inspired to explore what lies beyond self.

We sit deliberately, with noble posture and noble intention.

We mindfully breathe, allowing ease to arise. Progressively, we free our awareness from sensations. We free our awareness from the "I" we imputed upon the sensations and the "mine" with which we tried to claim them. We relieve ourselves of all of our mistaken identifications.

Breathing, we let go of the survival-based need to label all arisings. Dog barking, wind blowing, me meditating. We let go of the labels. Each gives rise to a story and a teller of the story.

Breathing, we relieve ourselves of the mental images with which we've formed and colored the arisings. We relieve ourselves of the clinging and aversion to the mental images of our own creation, the mental images which we believed to be external and thought would fulfill our neediness or hold our fear at bay, the mental images we hold responsible for our own reactive feeling tones.

Breathing, we relieve ourselves of our preconceptions and assumptions and beliefs, self-invested words we've imputed upon neural firings.

We completely let go of all that chaos and our attachment to and identification with it. We relieve ourselves of illusion-chasing and, cleared of all the congested weight of selfing, we enter surrender.

We just die into silence. Die to the past. Die to the future. Die to the breath. Completely let go. The silence reveals itself as refuge, as awareness that can be trusted, tender and resounding with the luminous quiet of mystery.

This silence is the practice of absorption, unruffled by even the breath of self, taught in all traditions. To practice it with the recognition that it is similar to the process of dying—to the impersonal process of leaving behind, becoming secluded from body and conceptual mind—is to amplify its power.

We will see clearly all of the places where we hold back, all of the places that bind us. This meditation is about letting go, surrendering. Each letting go is a death, an acknowledgement of the moment just passing, the moment that is no longer. We practice letting go with a deep understanding of why it is so important to let go. Releasing every prop, we let go into freedom. Releasing every fetter, we enter the quietly blissful relief of peace.

We engage in this practice in order to becoming familiar with the freedom that lies beyond grasping to self. It prepares us for dying and it opens us for living.

We will see, as we practice the meditation, the quick little mind of the ego looking for a loophole, any loophole, where it might continue, just as it is.

The sense of self believes it owns, is the possessor of, sensations, thoughts, feelings, and patterns. Just the reverse is so. Sensations, thoughts, feelings, and patterns give rise to the illusory sense of self. When they cease, so too does the sense of self. It will kick and scream, though, like a toddler being put to bed, mad at missing the party.

Engaging in the practice, over and over, on a frequent, rhythmic basis will allow us to become familiar with the laying down of self, with the surrender of pretense. It is wise and compassionate to do so.

THIS SPECIAL CONDITION of confronting our own mortality will be jet fuel for our practice. Buddha's observation was that meditation on death—confronting our own mortality, allowing ourselves to experience awareness without any reference to self—makes the deepest imprint on our minds, just as the elephant's footstep makes the deepest imprint on the ground.

To know awareness beyond selfing is to experience being without fear, perhaps for the very first time. Our fear of death is the same fear that keeps us so limited in our living. They are the same fear, the fear of death and the fear of living.

To know awareness beyond self, beyond its anchors of sensation and conception, is to be free from ignorance. With illusions undone, we are no longer separate. Fear disappears as we rest in communion. May we all experience the blessing of unselfconscious fearlessness.

WITHDRAWAL

LIBERATION FROM HABITS

> It is remarkable how easily and insensibly we fall into
> a particular route,
> and make a beaten track for ourselves. . . .
> The surface of the earth is soft and impressible by the feet of men;
> and so the paths with which the mind travels.
> How worn and dusty, then, must be the highways of the world,
> how deep the ruts of tradition and conformity!
>
> —Henry David Thoreau

Entering the later decades of our lives, we have already experienced a lessening of the overwhelming busy-ness of the lives we led when we were younger. The flood tides of hormonal surges and desires have receded to a more balanced level, allowing us glimpses of all that those waves had covered. Most of us can expect a lessening of the demanding and busy schedules we held as parents and/or as full-time members of the working world. There is a withdrawal from the fast pace and often empty challenges of workaday life as we've known it for the last many decades.

This is similar to the withdrawal people with terminal illness experience as their disease worsens. Withdrawal—a disengagement from busy-ness and its worldly, mindless persona—is one of the special conditions that arises at the end of life, enabling the spiritual transformation of the dying process.

For those of us without a catastrophic illness at the moment, though, our withdrawal is less extreme, less dramatic, less urgent than it would be if an illness were increasingly confining our lives and our activities. It is so much less, in fact, that we might miss the opportunity the withdrawal of aging offers if we don't keep our intention to spiritual ripen in the forefront of our minds.

THOSE STRUCTURES from which we are now released—alarm clocks and lunch breaks and weekdays and weekends—in many ways shaped the habits of our young adulthood and midlives. Insight can be easily obscured in the blurring frenzy of our busy-ness or deadened into numbness by the rut of our routines. Probably, for almost all of us, it was. As time sweeps us into the ranks of "old people," the necessity for the structures disappears.

With less frenzy to obscure our mindfulness, we are left with a more naked view of ourselves. We have slowed down enough for some keen observation. It's time, if we so choose, to fully make our own acquaintance, without the overlay of younger urges and midlife constraints and demands and schedules.

We retire from the outer rat race. This withdrawal offers us an opportunity to stop in our tracks, to halt in the rush of our headlong forward movement, and examine who we are and what we're doing.

What does Saturday mean when we don't have anywhere special to go on Wednesday either? What does it feel like to have fewer eyes on us, fewer eyes to trigger whatever needs we have to please or impress, whatever fears we have of judgment or rejection?

Aging brings changing relationships, changing abilities, and changing circumstances in its wake. They all offer the opportunity to change our priorities, to shuffle our deck of settled habits and settled routines and settled imperatives. There is no more need to put so much of our attention and energy into being a function. There is no more need to follow the insistence of "should," as so many of us have for so long.

Some of us have to cut through a lot of layers to even know what we want to do, so familiar are we with living robotically. There is real danger of depression and addiction if these years stretch before us as endless boredom, endless uselessness, if they stretch before us without a sense of purpose and a spiritual context.

Without the structures that held our young adult and midlife years in place, there is, in entering these later years, often a sense of release that can feel exhilarating or frightening or both. Many of us have no idea what to do with freedom. We often contract at the gate into endless possibility, pulling back a bit into the small but familiar comfort zone of the field we know.

Retirement from the pace of midlife places us on utterly new ground. We can feel put out to pasture, naked without the emperor's clothes of our previous position, wringing our hands with not enough to do to fill the hours. We can feel unneeded—a difficult experience for many of us whose self-worth depends primarily upon perceiving ourselves to be necessary, indispensable, to others. What a meat hook the word "indispensable" holds in its guise of goodness.

We may find a wasteland of loneliness, of boredom. We may wonder if this is all that lies ahead.

It is quite possible that we will find ourselves looking for distractions, escapes, from loneliness and boredom, the two lions at the gate of our oldest years. Let this looking for an escape be a red flag.

We can see that red flag on the cushion during meditation as we note the occasional boredom that arises with torpor and lack of clarity. We can see that red flag during meditation as we note the loneliness that often arises when we get a sense of the radical accountability that is demanded of us on a spiritual path. At times, we can feel utterly alone as we confront the depth of personal responsibility we have in the living of a life, in the transforming of a mind.

We can see our urge to dart away from loneliness, dash away from boredom, off the cushion, as well. If we remain mindful enough, intended enough, we will witness the various urges to fill the day, the urges to find a distraction, to "kill time."

Distraction is quite different from mindful engagement. Distraction is looking for another hiding place. We like our seemingly cozy corners of fiction and denial, often harboring them for quite a long while. Our ordinary mind is only too happy to welcome yet another opportunity to stay unmindful and play in the fields of its own mental images.

Many of us may find ourselves seeking to quickly fill this new emptiness on the calendar. It's like finding any seat we can in a game of musical chairs. "Please," we think, "don't let me end up without a chair, without a way to distract myself, without something to do, without someone to be with and to be with me, without feeling that this day matters and that I matter."

Some go to retirement communities where each day and night is filled with planned activity. Others search for some small thrill, an affirmation of personhood, in shopping. Golf can be raised to the level of religious ritual. And the addictive nature of the internet can create many a zombie, sitting motionless in a blue glow.

This is not to say that there is anything inherently wrong with retirement communities or planned activity, with shopping or golf or the internet. It is necessary to stay engaged, active, and connected to ensure our wellbeing during our later decades. It is a question of our intention as we engage in the actions that keep us connected with the world, with others, with nature, with wellbeing.

At this point in our lives, though, particularly if our intention is to spiritually mature, we need to learn to sit with some loneliness and boredom. We need to use the perspective those two conditions grant us to see what's going on inside. To be engaged in a spiritual path is to be in the process of weaning ourselves from the drama and distraction that we try to use as Band-Aids for loneliness and boredom.

THE EGO, at its height, wished to upgrade. We, as we age, have the opportunity to downsize. We can create some clearing of space, in both our inner and outer lives. Like hoarders whose houses are finally emptied, though, the temptation exists to fill them up again.

These aging years of ours, if we wish to use them wisely, are a time to be cautious. Caution with regard to how we fill this newly emptied time and space will allow us to explode into bold freedom, into deep and utter acceptance, into the simple enjoyment of being. Caution now with regard to our habits will allow us to achieve fearlessness in the face of both living and dying.

We need to stay on our toes with mindful questions, with meaningful questions. Are we simply living out the same habit patterns that have always run us? Are we running away from the opportunity for the thoughtful inquiry that this new ground, this newly acquired quiet and lessening of duties, seems to allow? Who am I if I'm not a function? Who am I without my habits? Who am I with less going on in my life that might reflect back a sense of self?

One friend, a retired professor, lives with her every day filled from morning to night, simply because she feels it "should" be. Her worth would be in question were it not. It is a powerful, deeply rooted habit, born seven decades ago. Another friend leaves herself at the mercy of politeness, of her fear of abandonment were she to say "no."

May we all have liberation from politeness. It will clear the way for the spontaneous and genuine, thoughtful and attentive loving-kindness that politeness attempts to portray.

Let's look at our orbits of devotion. Let's see if what we've been holding as central for so long is worthy of our devotion. Let's begin to cast out what isn't. Let's have no false gods before us. Let's engage this special condition of transformation—withdrawal—with mindfulness.

We want to examine the commitments we make in terms of our intention, in terms of whether or not they serve to liberate ourselves and others or to mire us more deeply in selfing. If our actions are idle and mindless, they're peripheral to our most noble and meaningful intention. They will keep us at the periphery of our being, chasing other intentions, seeking less reliable refuge. They will keep us, like a dog chasing its tail, following our own mistaken imaginings for the rest of our lives.

To dedicate these last years to awakening names their purpose and meaning—creates the pole star of each day. It changes our orbits of devotion and gives us more traction as we work to let go of old habits. Some of those habits can be as hard to turn around as a cruise ship in a small port. And sometimes our mindfulness is as small as the tiniest of tug boats.

A HELPFUL PRACTICE to incorporate in our lives, if we wish to use this remaining time to awaken, is the practice of intentional doing. Intentional doing is doing only what supports growing mindfulness and kindness and wisdom and compassion and joy. Such wise action fosters liberation from the unconscious habits of unmindful actions.

The practice of intentional doing includes plans we make for months away. We can ask ourselves, does this plan support my intention to awaken? Am I making this plan to reduce the itch of a passing restlessness? Do I intend the time to take a break from mindfulness, or do I intend to use the opportunity of the cruise, the visit, the commitment, to continue awakening, excluding nothing? The practice of intentional doing also includes the actions we take in each moment. Am I deliberately feeling each meeting of the foot with earth as I walk to the mailbox? Am I aware, in this moment, of formlessness functioning through this form? Am I *in* the experience of life?

Intentional doing, although holy work, is not somber work. Demanding great mindfulness at first, it leads us eventually to a life of simplicity and ease, free of resentment and conflict. It allows us, finally, to be more present, even lighter, in the face of the diminishments we encounter in our aging.

Usually, as we progress along a spiritual path, we begin to control our actions, our outward expression of inner habits, before we have the spiritual power of mindfulness to begin the task of taming their inner dynamics and freeing ourselves from them. Intentional doing allows us to manage our actions, to mindfully consider our intentions. It allows us to cause no harm. It allows us to practice kindness. It allows us to remain mindful of our actions and mindful of our intention.

Intention is everything. Are we with friends and family to forget or to remember? Are we volunteering to practice giving from a boundless heart or to feed our ego? Are we traveling to expand our embrace of all cultures and beings, to enjoy beauty, both natural and man-made, or to add feathers to our "well-traveled" cap? Is our motivation to numb or to grow and to share? The actions may outwardly appear the same.

With wise intention, the exact same actions that might have made us and those we encounter "less" can be infused with the light of ever-present awareness and all the gifts of spirit, freely shared. Spiritually maturing, practicing intentional doing, each action can leave us and all those we encounter "more"—more peaceful and more spacious, more free.

As our awareness becomes more refined, we can begin to notice a disenchantment, a disinterest, in actions and occasions filled with negativity in any of its thousand faces. In this further withdrawal, we begin to naturally gravitate, increasingly, toward what is sacred, toward what is good and true and beautiful.

We, if we are wise, will wean ourselves from negativity. We will, if we are wise, begin to wean ourselves from superficiality and meaninglessness.

ENDING THE OUTER RAT RACE gives us the opportunity to look at our inner rat race. This is where we work on training our own mind and freeing ourselves from the force fields of familiar assumptions and emotions.

Our habituated patterns of mind, well-worn neural pathways, are where we need to focus our looking if we want to reclaim the power that we have given them. Until we dismantle them, we are at their mercy. We have ignored the hidden imperatives of our own thoughts, words, and actions for a long time, relegating them to relative unconsciousness. Finally agreeing to no longer ignore them, we create the opportunity to be free of them.

Ken McLeod, whose teachings about habit patterns are insightful and precise, cautions that until the energy of our mindfulness is higher and more concentrated than the patterned energy of familiarity and habituation, our unconscious patterns will control us.

None of us would go to a young child for counsel on how to live a life. That is exactly what we do, though, when we allow our unexamined mental habit patterns with their beliefs and assumptions and attachments and aversions to hijack our awareness. We hand over the remote to our six-year-old selves.

These habit patterns of ours were formed when we were very young. They were brought into formation in a moment or series of moments long ago, in the initial distinctions of a separate sense of self. They have been acted upon in tens of thousands of moments since, each reenactment more deeply imprinting the pattern. These are the grooves upon which we impute our sense of "I."

Our unconscious patterned systems of concepts and associated emotions, self-referential to the core, were created by a child without enough information. They were created by a child with undeveloped capacity to see and to judge and to understand.

In many ways, ego can be described as the sum total of all of the defenses we created as children to avoid feeling hurt or frightened or forgotten. Our defenses form around wounds, ways in which we were hurt as children, ways in which we were harmed or neglected or simply took things personally. Just as the immune system gathers around a past attack in preparedness for a future attack of the same nature, so too do our defenses. They're rarely rational.

These defenses are our habit patterns. We equate them with our sense of self. How often have we had the thought, and even spoken it aloud, "that's just me—that's just the way I am"? We defend our habit patterns and egos, even though they were created in circumstances that no longer exist by children who no longer exist.

The conclusions that the young child came to about life, without the benefit of experience and wisdom, have determined in many ways the limitations in which we've lived for all these many years since. These foundational views of who we are, what life is like, what the world is like, what other people are like, and how we should be were formed six or seven decades ago.

Because these paradigms are so foundational in our psyche,

we rarely examine them. They are our unmindful "givens," the beliefs of our ignorance. We are not used to looking at our own expectations, assumptions, and predilections. We are unaware of our mind's amazing capacity to self-fulfill, to cause to "appear" these expectations, assumptions, and predilections.

We stay with what the six-year-old taught us. We see what we believe.

"The pressure's killing me. I feel like I'm going to explode. What should I do?"

"Hold it together. Muster up," says the six-year-old who watched his father suffocate behind his own wall, never sharing vulnerability.

"My marriage doesn't work. We're both unhappy. We're both smaller with each other. What should I do?"

"Stay, try harder, sacrifice yourself," says the six-year-old who tried to appease his quarreling parents, hungering for his vision of a happy home.

"I have cancer. Who can I turn to with all this fear and sadness?"

"Keep it to yourself; don't be a problem," says the neglected six-year-old who feels she must apologize for having needs.

IT'S TIME TO wisely and compassionately liberate the space of our elder years from the habit patterns of a child. Although we've long been cautioned not to "throw the baby out with the bathwater," in this instance—as we work on throwing out the bathwater of old habits—it's probably wise to throw the baby out, too.

Without mindful attention to our own thoughts and feelings, our aversions and attachments, and the daily stress of selfing, our reactions to the predictable sufferings of aging, loss, and illness will be out of our control. Our reactions will run blindly, governed by our habits. That is not a scenario anyone would mindfully choose.

We want to peel back the layers of these blind spots of unconsciousness and misconstrued paradigms. The task begins with bringing our own habits to light with mindfulness and managing them with some wisdom. This is like flying a helicopter, a more aerial, panoramic viewing stance, over those frenzied neural highways and recognizing that there is always an off-ramp.

Our habit patterns are most discernible at first on the cushion, in formal practice time. Although this is not necessarily the purpose of all formal practice time, before we can actually engage in each practice as the practice is intended, we need to see our own hindrances to practicing in an unimpeded, undistracted way.

Our habitual patterns of mind are our hindrances. They keep us bound within a flawed and mistaken paradigm. We will inevitably see our patterns as we sit. It could not be otherwise.

With whatever awakening practice we are employing, we simply sit and quiet the mind a bit, ingather attention a bit—these capacities will grow in time—and simply observe the mind wandering, noting where it wanders. We simply observe the dynamics of the movements of our own mind, the "unloading of the unconscious," as Thomas Keating puts it. We want to actually look. Actually see. This takes some doing. We've all, at one time or another, or perhaps many times, placed our bodies in the posture of looking while our mind was far away. We weren't looking at all.

With awakening our goal, this readiness to look, to explore what's actually going on in our minds, is a skillful approach. The ego seeks concealment. The growing confidence of a committed spiritual practice seeks to reveal. One wants darkness. One wants light.

We want to note the dynamics, the patterned ricochets, of our own karmic imprints. Sitting long enough, we'll see them begin to recycle over and over, like watching our clothes in a laundromat's dryer. There's that red shirt again.

THE FIRST STEP is recognizing the patterns. The stance is one of bare inquiry.

What are the thoughts and beliefs and habit patterns that have governed my experience of existing in the last day—or the last hour? Even more helpful—in this very moment as I sit here meditating? What stories am I telling myself—and believing—right here and right now?

Simply observe them. Habit patterns are like any system. They seek only to sustain themselves. They are impersonal. There is no self within them. Neither is there thought for the wellbeing of the self who believes his or her identity rests with them.

These systems are like a toy from the mid-twentieth century, when wind-up figures were popular. There was Jumping Joe, who jumped, and Dancing Debbie, who danced, and Marching Mike, who marched. You get the picture. Our habit patterns are just like these toys: wind them up, and they do what they do.

We all know anger in search of a target. We know the eagerness for praise, searching for credit or for approval. We've all experienced the run-rampant wish to control, just itching to jump in and show our better way. We've seen, in ourselves, the abject puddle of self-pity in search of someone, anyone, to cosign our victimhood. We've twisted in the longing that has the face of a bygone lover. We're familiar with the oppression of pleasing.

We all know sadness with its wet heaviness, its smooth and cleansing flow. We know anger with its mean thoughts, hoping to release the tension. Bruised feelings seeking comfort. Miserliness with its sense of "not enough." The downward spiral of despair. Grief that sears and stuns.

We all have some familiarity with fear, which hides in the braggadocio of denial or disappears into discouragement. Blaming, which satisfies the wish of not having to take responsibility. Jealousy, with its begrudging. Attachment, with its desperate clinging. We know the abject pain of self-judgment, like an ugly horned worm boring through ease.

Each habit pattern, an indifferent system, is looking for food to sustain itself.

These habit patterns are deeply ingrained and they condition every arising. They are our habitual escape routes, well-traveled paths of resistance to what is. They condition our perceptions of arisings over time and our perceptions of arisings in each nanosecond. It is in the nanosecond where we begin to look at them.

Seeing what it is that we're bound in, we can more skillfully unbind ourselves. We want to see the habits—hear their voices, feel their fears, sense their imperatives. They are what we've believed and embodied for all of these years. It is wise to pay attention and to question.

ALTHOUGH FOR DECADES we have placed our sense of self upon our habit patterns, like a lunar capsule landing on the moon, with mindfulness we can begin to dis-identify from these rutted grooves, the impersonal systems of our mental habits. Not identified, we can begin to practice nonreactive equanimity as they arise. They will be seen for what they are. It's a bit like watching ginger ale go flat.

Over and over, we return to the seat, with growing humility and patience and determination, and allow ourselves to be present with these arisings with less and less reactivity. With intention and practice and increasing insight, we grow in that ability. With increasing insight, we are measurably less inclined to give the habit pattern quarter, to allow it to take form.

As we begin, it is helpful to have hints as to where to look. We are so used to our own habit patterns that we don't even recognize them initially. We're used to being fairly unconscious, unmindful. Most of us have sleepwalked through a lot of decades.

Buddhist wisdom speaks of the eight worldly concerns, the eight places where we typically get hooked out of the present, right out of bare awareness, and back into story. Our ego is a huge dust collector. These eight worldly concerns, the traps that keep us enmeshed in reactivity, are loss and gain, pleasure and pain, fame and shame, praise and blame. These are eight good places to begin looking.

We may have witnessed our own habitual reactions to loss and gain, hating one and loving the other, as we've watched our retirement accounts take a roller coaster ride. We can see which of the eight sirens has lured us in when we're concerned about our aging appearance or have too much pride to use a cane or a walker if we need one. We may witness our reactions if and when we're faced with a death of a loved one, faced with the new reality of having to weather the years of old age alone, or faced with finding ourselves propped up in one of the wheelchairs that line the halls of every nursing home. We'll witness it as we meet with the doctor to hear the results of a test. Every ounce of our being will rise or fall with the words "positive" or "negative."

There are so many places to get snagged, to further congest the free flow of life. Remembering the eight worldly concerns is like remembering to bring a map of the waters when we go out in a boat. There are shoals everywhere. It is good to ask ourselves, often, can I let go? Can I pry my attachment loose, like an old stubborn lid on a dusty jar? Am I willing to completely and utterly let go of all of these deceptions and the power I give them?

Our habit patterns exist in a dream state. They don't care about awakening. They're like teenagers who only want to sleep.

WITH MINDFULNESS, we can watch the urge of a habituated pattern and not follow it. We can watch the beliefs of a habit pattern and not believe them. We can watch the grasping of the "I," so invested in landing within the habit pattern, so itching to plant a flag. We can relax the grasping.

What shift can I make in this moment to live more lightly? With more ease? With more gratitude? How can I shift my view, right now, into a kinder heart? Into more clarity? What are the resistances and snags that are keeping me enmeshed and entangled in this congestion of my own creation right now?

Bringing into consciousness what has been unconscious is a significant part of walking a spiritual path. It reduces the gap between our highest glimpses and most noble aspirations, and the mindless, familiar patterns that actually live our daily lives for us. These imprints keep us trapped in the narratives we've both woven from our habituations and used to explain them. They keep us trapped in awareness that has no access to light and to wisdom.

We are way too far along in years to continue to allow ourselves to be run by anything other than our own deliberated aspirations and intentions, by anything other than our most noble qualities. Our mindfulness may need maturing and ripening in order to stably abide in them, but those noble qualities are always, already, in each of us. We each have a buddhanature, a Divine Indwelling.

Enough of squandering. Enough of acting childishly, immaturely, in a wrinkled old body. Enough of cheating ourselves of the fullness of this human life. We alone are responsible. There is no dodging that total accountability.

It's time to do some pruning. We prune in accordance with wisdom and intention. Pruning unmindfulness, mindfulness grows.

Pruning, we keep what's essential. We allow for new growth. We allow for beauty.

To prune is to let go, to no longer feed habituated patterns with the energy of our attention, to choose more beneficial options.

We want to discriminate between which of our thoughts and actions and habitual patterns are helpful in terms of awakening and which keep us asleep. We want to discern which are beneficial and which are harmful. This discernment is wisdom. Wisdom is without the blurring weight and the obstructing emotional reactivity of selfing.

We need some skillful means at this juncture. When we begin to become mindful of the addictive patterns of thoughts and emotions that have held sway in our experience of life, it often feels a bit like discovering ourselves to be tied in endless knots. Buddha described the experience as feeling "smothered and enveloped like a tangled skein, a knotted ball of string."

We can expect that many times in our practice it can feel a bit overwhelming to see how deep and entangled are the imprints of unconsciousness. We may note old habits of judgment that tell us we can't do this, old habits of laziness that would have us drop the whole notion of awakening and walk away, old habits of discouragement or frustration or unworthiness.

With a knotted tangle of yarn or rope or string, if we pull too tightly or impatiently, the knots just become knottier, more tightly entangled. Similarly, if we begin to judge ourselves as we witness the thicket of our own addictive patterns of thoughts, or push back down what we are noticing, the tangle of each habit system just becomes more difficult to see and more difficult to undo.

Best to untangle ourselves skillfully and compassionately. Best to patiently, and with gratitude and even with a sense of joy and growing confidence, take the time to clearly see each intricate entanglement so that we can unwind, unbind, from it. These are the knots that have bound us for decades and caused us great confusion and stress. The knots are habitual patterns born of traumas, losses, disappointments, prides, jealousies, comparisons, judgments, hurts, fears. They're filled with unconscious should's and must's. In the end, they're nothing but neural firings to which we've added congested layer upon congested layer of embroidered stories and imperatives.

Confronting the tangled mass of interwoven patterns, we isolate one at a time—the one presently arising—and simply open to it. We allow ourselves to inquire into its thoughts, convictions, associated emotions and sensations. They all arise and abide and dissolve. We simply witness. Increasingly seen, the power of these systems, these habit patterns held in unconsciousness, begins to dissipate. Utterly seen, the plug is pulled on their power completely.

We can apply antidotes, as we begin our journey, if we get hijacked by a pattern. Any of the noble qualities of our essential nature, the qualities of grace, can neutralize the mental afflictions. We simply, in visionary Ken Wilber's words, add creativity to karma. We cultivate a mind such as patience or generosity or lovingkindness, recognizing it as a more beneficial mind in which to be than the mind of any of the mental afflictions. This is wise. We cannot hold two minds at the same time, regardless of how good we might think we are at multitasking.

That the pattern appears to our mind makes it our responsibility to manage. But responsibility is not the same as shame or blame. And managing it simply means healing the wounds that gave rise to it. Managing it simply means opening to it, inquiring into it, and working through it. There is no other way to come unbound. We all need to find our own way home. The way home is through our own thickets, saving the only life we can save.

We all have the whole panoply of the limiting afflictions of a human mind, which has seven billion permutations. If everyone was unfamilar with the minds of fear and pride and the other mental poisons, if these weren't universal afflictions of the human mind, we wouldn't even have words for them. It is important to remember that although we are responsible for managing them since it is our mind in which they appear, who we are in our essential nature is not the habit patterns of a lifetime's mindless accumulation.

When we allow unbinding from our patterns, whether they be patterns of grasping and clinging or patterns that give rise to great aversion, the noble qualities of our essential nature are no longer obscured. This unbinding, arising out of skillful mindfulness and compassion, leaves us not only more harmless to ourselves but more harmless to all we encounter. The world is in sore need of more harmless presences.

Compassion is needed to do this work. To simply discern a pattern is the practice. We simply accept, as openly and peacefully as we can, each arising as what is in each moment and, then, let go of our reactivity to it. It will naturally atrophy when we are no longer feeding it with attention and story. We all know, having uncovered our relentless habits, how much suffering we have endured under the control of each of them. We know how many words that we regret saying, how many words we regret not saying, how paltry was our love and concern at times, how much we've missed of joy and connection in the trance of self-absorption.

The practice of exploring and freeing ourselves from unconsciousness is not about judging ourselves in the mistaken belief that we are the pattern or about becoming discouraged because the habit pattern lingers. We've already suffered enough at its hands. Our commitment to practice deserves our tenderness, always gently but firmly nudging a fuller opening to depth. Our commitment to practice deserves our respect, not the revival of our old tendencies to judge or the well-worn tumble into giving up. We are all works in progress.

These habit patterns, essentially, are familiar neural firings, centered in rather primitive parts of our brain, the hidden harbors of the mental poisons that beset us all. Compassion, for others and for ourselves, rewires those neural firings of habits, the source of so much suffering, ushering attention to areas of the brain more capable of sustaining equanimity and caring and clarity. Our brains are simply vehicles for formless awareness to function in form. It is kind and wise to learn to use them well.

With mindfulness, applied earnestly and steadfastly, the patterns begin to become recognizable more quickly. The Dharma lag decreases. We can begin to see through the habits. Their sharp edges fade. They begin to appear and to be experienced as more ethereal, less substantial. As this happens, we usually also begin to witness the sense of self, now also coming into awareness as an object of observation.

There is a natural progression to this transformative process. We see the self's habits, first, before we see the habit of selfing.

As we engage in a growing mindfulness practice, a practice of inquiry, our experience, at first, is of the self observing arising appearances. As we become more adept at concentrated looking, we enter deeper levels of subtlety. Awareness begins observing the self who believes itself to be observing the karmically determined appearances. Awareness notes "selfing" as a localized reference point—simply another arising appearance, the appearance most frequently reiterated, our most consistent interference with clear seeing.

It takes a long time before we can see the habit pattern of selfing, before we can witness the witness. That capacity to abide in awareness that observes the self selfing heralds a big shift. All of our work with habit patterns has been preparation for working with this one, the mother of all habit patterns.

We can see that we presume a self. We presume others. We presume environments and externality. We presume the sacred as separate, as other, and both fear and long for it. We can observe not only our sensations and emotions and thoughts as they emerge in habituated systems, we can begin to discern the self believing it to be an inherently existing possessor of these fleeting, patterned movements of sensations and emotions and thoughts.

Stepping back, to the degree of being able to witness the belief in the self, allows us to recognize that it is not so much the movements of the mind that are problematic. It is the belief in the self as creator of those movements, possessor of those movements, victim of those movements, or accomplisher of those movements that is problematic. To clearly and stably see selfing as simply another habit pattern destroys the power that believing endowed upon selfing. Seeing zaps self-grasping. It sets awareness free.

No longer so caught and befuddled, we can engage more and more spontaneously in intentional doing. Removing selfing's interference, we can begin to allow formlessness to function through form, to simply *be* within their unity, with both gratitude and grace.

SILENCE

LIBERATION FROM ILLUSIONS

> If we were not so single-minded
> about keeping our lives moving,
> and for once could do nothing,
> perhaps a huge silence
> might interrupt this sadness
> of never understanding ourselves
>
> —Pablo Neruda

Most of us live in way too much noise. This is a busy, clamoring, tumultuous world, and we, for the most part, have busy, clamoring, tumultuous minds.

We need to create havens of quiet.

Silence is a solace. It is a space of penetrative relaxation, like falling into a hammock and, feeling ourselves to be suspended and supported, allowing ourselves to be suspended and supported. We can sink into it and let go of all of the tension and energy required to hold up both ourselves and our stories. Quietude gives us a deep rest.

SILENCE IS ONE of the special conditions that facilitates the awakening we seek. It arises naturally as we come to the end of life, closer to active dying and our very last breaths. The impulse to talk decreases, the strength to talk weakens, the desire to speak anything but the most essential communication diminishes.

It's enormously helpful to begin to cultivate silence while still in the midst of life. This transformative special condition helps us to spiritually ripen.

Many wisdom traditions, religious orders, monasteries, and convents have adopted the practice of outer silence precisely because it does allow us to cultivate interior silence. Interior silence is a rich mind to cultivate. It is the relaxed and nonreactive state of mind that is both the calling card and the benefit of having done some deep awakening work.

Truth be told, as works in progress, we have conflicting urges: the urges to awakening and the urges of the ego. Often, we find that we both love silence and that we're afraid of it. When we find a moment or an hour of silence in a woods or by the sea or just inside our own little home, we relish it—but not for too long. Restlessness kicks in. The desire for a little drama, a little entertainment, kicks in, and we follow the urge.

SILENCE CAN BE FRIGHTENING. The absence of noise can be deafening. Refraining from speech can block ego's desire to frolic in one of its favorite amusement parks.

Outward quiet, the absence of noise and the refrainment from speech, lifts the veil on the constant chatter going on in our minds. There's often a fear that we'll get lost or engulfed if we don't distract ourselves, a fear that we'll go mad in the craziness of our own minds. Many people carry the fear that if they open to their wounds and touch the deep wells of sorrows and hurts that they've kept contained in their psyches, those sorrows and hurts may be all they'll ever experience, exclusively and eternally. This is not so. We've been crazy, but not in the way we think.

Although we're usually unaware of it, especially if we have not yet begun to cultivate an awakening practice, our minds are constantly filled with the noise of our own inner monologue. It's a twenty-four-hour talk show in there, unmonitored, uncensored. Although the monologue has no allegiance to reality whatsoever, we believe and react to every word. Our patterns run rampant in words, like kids in a classroom when the teacher steps out for a moment.

Weaning ourselves from automatically believing our own thoughts is an initial project if we wish to awaken. It requires mindful investigation and the wisdom to let go and skill in doing so.

Weaning ourselves from believing in our emotions as validations of the truths of our beliefs is a necessary step, as well. It requires, also, mindful observation and skill in soothing and releasing the unease. This weaning becomes easier when we don't identify with or feel that we possess what's happening. We grow in our realization that awareness has no concept of self or preferences, no concepts at all.

If we wish to awaken, we need to wean ourselves from mindlessly following the lead of habit patterns that were created by that six-year-old within us, who has insufficient information and undeveloped capacity for judgment. Such habit patterns have no regard for our happiness—only for their own viability.

AWAKENING AS WE AGE is a process of letting go, of offering up our previously cherished stories and illusions. It begins with a growing moment-by-moment willingness to let go of who we think we are for the sake of all that lies beyond that thought.

Our practice helps us to keep from being continuously reborn in old habit patterns. Our committed practice can keep us from bouncing around unconsciously from desire to desire, believing our interpretative thoughts about what's actually happening. Neurons fire; we add words.

Our inner monologue is constant. Every word in it, each noise of it, is self-referential. Every moment of its ongoingness sustains our illusion of self.

How we would hate it if we had to wear some device on our heads that would pick up the thoughts of our inner monologues and broadcast those thoughts far and wide. How we would hate to have that ceaseless chorus of words overheard. Can you imagine? In the waiting room in a doctor's office? In line at the supermarket? As we sit on our front porch, for the whole neighborhood to hear? Endless, meaningless words that would astonish us—and those around us—with their absurdity, the pettiness of their views. Judgmental, comparing words that would embarrass us with their ignorance. Fearful, needy, preening, grasping words—all self-referential. Ego would begin to monitor the chatter just to spare itself the humiliation.

Outer silence allows us to sit with this internal monologue. The noisy stream of consciousness, without the mindfulness of a transformative practice, is ceaseless in its continuous weaving of the sense of self over an edgy abyss of ignorance.

To sit with the internal monologue, in equanimity and with patience, with a view that's unwavering, allows the inner noise to quiet, to sputter out, to still. Not overnight, but in time, with steadfast commitment to overcome the downhill slip of mindfulness into unconscious, habituated believing, we can still the noisiness of selfing.

This is the path to liberation from illusions—freedom from attachment to the self, seen finally as the illusory creation of a congested snarl of countless ingrained, noisily compelling habits of mind.

To ADOPT OUTWARD SILENCE, as a special condition that facilitates awakening over time, quiets the internal monologue. In a quiet mind, attention finds release from the mistaken conclusions of the mind's noisiness. An utterly quiet mind and a self cannot coexist.

We learn to be silent by being silent. We create inner silence when we practice outer silence. One retired friend, who dedicated a day each week to silence, shared that just that dedicated practice carved a lot of other "craziness" out of his life. He felt it brought him back to basic sanity and natural simplicity.

With the practice of outer silence, we are able to sit longer and longer in inner silence. We sit, like a woman on a widow's walk—in silence, waiting patiently and lovingly and with yearning for the beloved. Centered and unwavering. Alert and intent upon her purpose, on seeing the top of that tall, white mast on the horizon.

Interior silence allows us to be receptive to insight and allows us to remain mindful of intention. It empties the mind and, in that emptying, allows us the experience of grace.

Silence is not just the absence of noise. It is an affirming presence of our essential nature, beyond words. Our essential nature has for so many of us for so many years been obscured by words. Just as the absence of attachment to ego does not lead us to a void of nothingness but into the radiant presence of naked awareness, inner silence does not lead us to nullity but to fullness. It is not a "no" but a "yes."

THERE ARE TWO WAYS we can implement the special condition of silence as we engage in the task of ripening into spiritual maturity. Silence is a seed that we can plant in the field of awakening. We can, if we choose, practice both noble silence and essential silence.

Noble silence, like the Grand Silence of many religious orders, is total abstinence from speaking for a specified period of time. To practice noble silence for a part of each day—or even just for an afternoon each week—leads us inward. It keeps us on the trajectory of our intention.

On retreat, for example, we practice noble silence. Understanding the meaningfulness of the insights of our sessions and the relatively more peaceful minds in which we have abided during our sessions, we deliberately refrain from dribbling away the power of the mind of absorption. With noble silence, we don't squander the ingathered attention that is engaged in awakening. We don't waste it in frivolousness, in idle chatter that draws our attention out of absorption, diluting and scattering it, bequeathing it back to ignorance.

In noble silence, we don't engage in conversation at all. The choice to do this arises from the recognition that most conversation, unless we practice with great mindfulness or the selflessness that arises out of the minds of love and compassion, pops us right back into selfing.

The choice to keep noble silence for periods also arises out of the recognition that to maintain silence, as a deliberate discipline, keeps us in remembrance and awareness of the holy. Noble silence keeps our minds free from the noise that obscures recognition of the sacred.

If we do choose to engage in the practice of noble silence each day, we simply pick the time parameters for this practice. We inform the people around us of our intention and our decision, and we resist our own urges to engage in speaking during that specified time.

Essential silence, the other silence practice, is to speak only as appropriate, only if it is essential. Essential silence is a practice that we can maintain throughout each day, all day long.

It could be said that essential silence demands even more mindfulness than noble silence. We can think of the experience of a person who is on a diet, for example, whose eating is restricted to only a few well-chosen foods in only a few prescribed amounts. The directions are clear and, after a while, the dieter can simply think of everything that is not on the diet as "not food," "not available for consumption." Such dieting is comparable to noble silence.

Off the diet and engaged more in weight management than in dieting, decisions about eating become trickier. The choices are more subtle because the field to range in is wider. This is similar to how it is with essential silence. It is tricky to decide, with the wily ego ever ready to slip in, what is necessary to say, what is appropriate. Great mindfulness and great alertness are required. Essential silence trains us in discernment.

Essential silence demands that we begin to use discriminating wisdom as to when to speak and when not to. It demands that we know our intention in either speaking or not speaking, that we know our intention in what we choose to say. Essential silence is neither cold nor aloof. It is not fearful.

Are we being quiet to withhold? Are we avoiding a challenge or avoiding taking a stance? Are we remaining silent because speaking would demand greater courage? Are we silent in fear or in denial or in separation? Are we speaking in service to self or are we speaking in service to awakening? We need to examine our intention in as many moments as we can. If our intention and attention are not aligned with our wish to awaken, we simply bring them back and straighten up, back into present-centered awareness.

To INCORPORATE the special condition of essential silence into our commitment to spiritually mature as we age doesn't mean that we can only ask for the butter to be passed or mention that the house is on fire.

It doesn't mean that we don't talk to each other. Of course we want to share and open our hearts and talk from our hearts with each other. Of course we want to laugh and sing. Laughing and singing bring us to joy. We want to offer our playfulness as a currency of love.

Essential silence is warm and embracing. It is inclusive and connected. When speech occurs, it is honest and authentic and direct. When speaking is appropriate, it entails speaking soul to soul, essence to essence. Jane Eyre described it when she proclaimed to Rochester, "I am not speaking to you from mortal flesh."

When we are centered in that mind of warm and embracing essential silence, we respond appropriately. We share, we encourage, we touch each other and connect. Practicing essential silence is a profound act of generosity, a profound act of a boundless heart.

There is a beautiful iconographic image of the buddha Tara in the Tibetan Buddhist tradition. She is the embodiment of the protective aspects of enlightenment and sits, unlike the cross-legged postures of all of the other holy beings, with one leg extended, ever ready to help. Her intention to assist is so powerful that, if she is needed, she doesn't even want to have to take the time to uncross her legs from the *vajra* posture. It is in this mind without self-reference that we engage in essential silence.

ESSENTIAL SILENCE IS an especially skillful practice. It stops us from engaging in the idle chatter that reinforces the illusions of self and others. It keeps us from dissipating our energy and engaging in one of ego's most familiar and habituated drugs of choice: mindless speaking. Essential silence cultivates the inner quiet that is the crucible of transformation.

Essential silence allows us to appreciate the profound gift of speech. We take the gift of speech so utterly for granted.

Tongue and mouth and teeth and larynx and lungs function together to make sounds. That we can hear these sounds with our ears, that our minds can make words of the sounds, that the words have meaning, that we can understand, with our hearts, and share invisible thoughts and feelings with another is nothing short of a miraculous gift.

To RECOGNIZE the gift of speech as sacred and the gift of listening as sacred keeps us within the mind of essential silence.

As our inner silence grows, we begin to recognize, as did Annie Dillard, the American poet and contemplative, that "the silence is all there is." Martin Laird speaks of "the silent land of our own being" and the deep call of that silence.

Out of that silence arise essential words—kind words, wise words.

We need to rest in formless awareness in order to function in form without getting lost in it, to use functioning in form well and wisely. In the same way, we need to rest in silence for these essential words of kindness and wisdom to be uttered in our own minds and in the world and to one another.

In inner silence, we remain in communion and in remembrance. As we deepen our stability in inner silence, distractions no longer enchant us. We hold ourselves open inwardly, both to receive and to share. We hold ourselves as space, silent and still. Liberated from our illusions, silence enables movement out of attachment to consensual reality. There is a deactivation of the worldly persona, the mental image that ego believes it portrays to the world and imagines that the world perceives. There is an atrophying of the very emotional and mental habituations that juggled and maintained the sense of self and made it feel real.

Rodney Smith, a brilliant Dharma teacher, points out that the spiritual journey could be described as the movement from noise to silence. As the internal monologue is slowed and diminished, the emptying of the mind begins. There is an emergence of the "still small voice within." The state of natural great peace is uncovered as selfing's obscurations thin.

Attention becomes more absorbed. It comes to rest in awareness that is concentrated, still, present. This allows for the emergence of illuminated insight or wisdom.

We enter the mind of wordless prayer. We recognize, in deep inner silence, that it is impossible for language and words to contain reality, that reality lies where words end. In this nonconceptual, postverbal mind of inner silence, we encounter reality directly—the humming of life, of being, silently resounding. Released from attachment to self, we begin to see no difference in the nature of empty mind and moving mind. This is the freedom of inner silence. It remains unruffled regardless of arisings.

Just as we enter love by being love, we enter silence by being silence. A warm, embracing, very present silence. A refuge. The ultimate old-age home.

SOLITUDE

LIBERATION FROM ATTACHMENT; RELEASE INTO SUFFICIENCY

> There is grace and love
> in this lonely growth process
> that unwinds and unwheels me.
> . . . There is a new freedom . . .
> that excites me with its
> unknowingness.
>
> —Bonnie Shultz

One of the circumstances that arises at the time of dying, a circumstance that contributes to the transformative experience of dying, is solitude. We are increasingly alone in our own being as we come close to death.

At the time of our dying, we are at a deep remove from those around us. Even if we're surrounded by other dying people, even in a plane crash or a tsunami or a battlefield or a hospice house, we are utterly alone in our own dying. For most people, in particular for those without some kind of awakening practice, without some kind of felt and trusted spiritual compass in their lives, the loneliness that arises as we come close to death can be hard to endure.

How much kinder we would be to ourselves, how much wiser, if we were to have already transformed loneliness into aloneness, far before the time of our death. We effect this transformation by touching and tasting and continuing to nourish ourselves in the richness available in solitude.

LONELINESS IS an experience of the pain of our own conceived separateness, undernourished by spirit. It is an experience of deficiency. In it, we think and feel that we are not sufficiently cared for or cared about, not sufficiently supported, not sufficiently in connection. We feel not sufficient, period.

In loneliness, we feel the absence of the attention of others. We feel a loss of all that we would wish to find in the eyes and company of others—validation, praise, acceptance. For some, our reflection as we perceive it in the eyes of others may be our only proof that we exist.

Loneliness appears choiceless. It has the sense of something missing, of insufficiency. It is disempowering and can mire us more deeply in self. One friend, single, in her seventies with no family, shared that she felt a sense of absolute loneliness that often left her terrified and sobbing. She wondered, at the time, if continuing to exist were worth it. Loneliness is a hell.

Loneliness is the experience of being alone through a lens of deficiency and aversion, through the lens of ignorance.

Aloneness, outwardly, appears similar to loneliness: the same circumstance of seclusion from others. In the experience of aloneness, though, the solitude is viewed through the lenses of gratitude and openness. The condition of solitude is recognized as having been made—or accepted—as an act of wise and beneficial choice.

Solitude, accepted and chosen, is rich and transformative. It has a sense of fullness, wholeness, sufficiency. Solitude is a sweet and fulfilling enclosure of aloneness. That sense of sufficiency is profoundly empowering. It enables us to pursue our spiritual aspirations with continuously growing confidence.

Both loneliness and aloneness are states of mind, generated by two quite different perspectives.

The more spacious of the two perspectives, that of aloneness, is engendered in solitude. It arises in the real work, the holy work, that we do on a spiritual path. It arises as we increasingly release ourselves from the gravitational pull of our attachments. It is generated as we free ourselves from believing that our happiness is contingent upon anything other than our own awareness.

Aloneness comes to be seen as a necessary condition to create in our lives if we are ever to see through the illusions of our own mind and attain the spiritual maturity that makes this time of our later years so precious and meaningful and urgent.

At the time of death, the solitude of seclusion is needed to let go, to ingather, to surrender, to make the leap into awareness beyond self. In the midst of life, chosen periodic seclusion appears to be a necessity as well, if we wish to move beyond painful emotional reactivity into awareness liberated from attachment to self and to the mental images, the imagined worlds, of selfing.

This special condition of seclusion, the cultivation of solitude, has been adopted by many a wisdom tradition precisely because of its facilitation of transformation. Vision quests, solitary caves and huts, cloisters, and solo retreats, for example, all arose as ways to bring seclusion into the spiritual path, recognizing it as a special condition that hastens awakening.

> And don't we all, with fierce hunger,
> crave a cave of solitude,
> a space of deep listening—

> full of quiet darkness and stars,
> until finally we hear a syllable of God
> echoing in the cave of our hearts?
> —MACRINA WEIDEKEHR

To make a commitment to incorporate some periodic solitude in our lives both signals and amplifies our investment in our intention to awaken.

Our spiritual practice will not mature if it stops at entertaining the thought of spiritual practices. It will not mature if it stops at reading and listening and conceptually understanding. Our spiritual practice will never ripen if it stops at longing.

We must apply what we learned from our study of wisdom traditions to this very mind that conceptually understands the words we've studied. We need to churn information into transformation. We are going to have to take our longing and fill the whole of our being with it, not just our head. We need to embody our intention if we wish to awaken into awareness beyond self.

Solitude allows us the necessary time and space away from others to build and deepen our capacity to awaken. The poet Mary Oliver reminds us of the old poet-monks of China, who fled the world and its busy-ness, disappearing into the mists of mountains. Solitude allows us to develop the platform, the stability of insight, from which we can attain liberation from attachment to all the once and perhaps still enchanting seductions.

THE CHOSEN TIME in solitude presents us with temporary disengagement from much of the world of sensory and sensual distractions and our reactive attachments to them. In seclusion, without our ordinary parade of entertainments, we can effect significant growth in mindfulness.

We can effect growth in the stability of our focused awareness.

We make it possible to see, with great clarity, the limiting and peace-disturbing patterns of our own mind. They are dizzying and exhausting. Alone, in solitude, we can grow in our capacity to simply witness the ramblings with some measure of growing dispassion and growing detachment. This bare witnessing holds within itself no obstructions.

In solitude, we can step off the tracks for a while as a deliberate antidote to the habituated following of our mind's own seductive routes.

Seclusion allows us to remove ourselves from the pace and noise and crowdedness of the ordinary day and week in this culture. Until it is well stabilized, our mindfulness has a tendency to thin when we're going at a fast pace, to diminish in interactions with others. Interaction with others is an arena in which the ego loves to play.

Except for the singularly alone moments that we will encounter—moments of aging and sickness and grieving and death—solitude is often a hard commodity to come by. Even for those who are lonely, or feel alone even in relationship, solitude as a positive experience is not typically cultivated in our world. We live in a world of the internet, a global village with round-the-clock news. There is no solitude, unless we incorporate it into our own lives deliberately, until we designate it as such and choose it.

We may find loneliness easily enough, but where will we find solitude in the assisted living facility or the nursing home? Where will we find solitude with a caregiver in the house? In the hospital or living with our kids and grandchildren? It exists as a state of mind to cultivate in our own being. We cultivate it by incorporating some of the outward circumstances of seclusion into our lives with the intention that the inner experience of quiet sufficiency, lessened attachment, will ensue.

To adopt the practice of solitude from time to time removes us temporarily from all of the places and all of the activities and all of the people where we habitually seek a happiness that we believe to be externally contingent. In this reprieve, some of these patterned ways in which we ordinarily react to the arisings in our lives so robotically and in such a deadened way have an opportunity to simply sputter out of fuel.

Less controlled by the habits and beliefs that deaden us, we can return, after solitude, to engagement, to connection. Importing the practice of seclusion into our lives on a deliberate and rhythmic basis allows for renewal, for refreshment. Upon our return to the increased stimuli of a busier world than the world we experienced in our solitude, we can respond anew, respond freshly, less reactively, with each moment's new arisings.

Who would not want to return to the world with each moment fresh? To resist the impulse to paint endless, deadened sameness onto our present and onto our future? To meet each person, even our known and beloved, even our known and disliked, even who we have believed ourselves to be, anew? To realize, with wonder and appreciation, that we have never before experienced the moment now arising?

We can use seclusion to return to the world with more clarity, less preconception, and less expectation. Much of this clarity arises from growing detachment, a growing zero-ing in on purpose, a growing intention.

We begin to see what no longer supports our expanded awareness and our amplified intention. We wean ourselves. Aging is an often painful process of weaning. The mind intending toward spiritual maturity is a mind that can appreciate the liberation that weaning offers.

Solitude and silence appear as similar special conditions. Seclusion or solitude has many of the same consequences as the practice of silence. They're both akin to the withdrawal that begins to occur naturally as we enter our older years.

In the practice of silence, what is eliminated is noise, both outer and inner. In the practice of solitude, what is eliminated is the busyness of espying movement, the activity of human beings, the sight of others, the dazzling displays of the marketplace.

One practice works with our capacity to hear, the other with our capacity to see.

Simplifying our visual field, in seclusion, we can more clearly see our attachments. Attachments come into stronger focus when they are not satisfied. Solitude can help us recognize and thin our attachment to visual appearances as distractions, as objects to grasp or to push away, and as illusory proofs of who we think we are.

It is a powerful recognition when, through the practice of silence, we hear the voices of our own habituated inner monologues, those basically boring tapes, continuously recycling, and recognize that we no longer need to believe the words or the feelings. Equally, it is a powerful recognition when we realize, through the practice of solitude, that all we have ever witnessed are our own mental images. In the intentionally simplified circumstance of solitude, with visual appearances reduced and minimized, we can begin to see into our own projecting. We can begin to see that our entire story and struggle, with all of the attachments and aversions, have been in reaction to nothing but our own mental images, our own constructed caricatures.

SIGHT IS PERHAPS the strongest of our senses, the one upon which we rely the most. It seems to provide the most continuously convincing evidence that there is an external world that exists exactly as it appears.

We can experience the changing impermanence of fleeting bodily sensations—a sneeze arising, reaching crescendo, releasing, for example. We can experience an itch begin, abide, and cease. We can hear and recognize the ephemerality of sound. We can even, with much practice and the mindfulness developed with that practice, experience the changing, shifting nature of the sensations of chronic pain.

On the other hand, phenomena apprehended visually, without a continuous mindful recognition of impermanence, always seem more enduring, more solidly and convincingly form. Eyes cannot contact formlessness.

We arise from meditation and the wall in front of where we've been sitting still appears to be the wall in front of where we've been sitting. The wall always appears to be the wall. We walk outside, and the tree and the road always appear to be the tree and the road. They always appear to be solidly there. It's convincing. We're easily convinced.

Ordinary appearances have a functional necessity, and it is deeply ingrained in our thinking to *believe* ordinary appearances. We believe that things exist as they appear. We live, unconsciously, within that paradigm. We have attachment to that paradigm.

We may know that our eyes are actually only capable of registering light wave refractions—not of "seeing" walls and trees and roads. But the tendency is very strong, very ingrained, to forget—once we apply labels to those light wave refractions—that we are witnessing walls and trees and roads only as they exist as images in our mind.

In seclusion, we can begin to see this dynamic with clarity. The inner cinema gets released full force when the outer cinema lessens. We can begin to detach from the myriad ways we have taken it all to exist independently of our own mind. We can begin to detach from all of the myriad ways that we have reacted to our own mental images and imputations.

THESE RECOGNITIONS ALLOW for growing detachment. This is not the detachment of coldness and aloofness and indifference. This is the detachment of liberation from attachment. We need not fear not loving as our attachment decreases. Our love just increases; it is no longer obstructed by the self-referential quality of attachment. Love, the mind that wishes another to be happy, the mind of deeply grateful appreciation, blossoms unimpeded in detachment.

It could be said that seclusion, solitude, is an absolutely necessary condition for awakening into awareness beyond self. All transformation, liberation from self, occurs alone, in our own singular awareness. Where else could it occur? With intention and committed practice, we can come to increasingly live in the less personalized, less reactive, more detached recognition that our idea of self rests as a mere appearance within formless awareness.

Paradoxically, in order to stop taking everything personally, we need to make our spiritual practice very personal. Initially, we need to use the self as a tool to free awareness from selfing.

It is a powerful step on anyone's spiritual path when we thoroughly and completely understand that the only transformation possible is the transformation of our own unique minds. We don't need to be perfect to attain liberation. We don't need to erase our uniqueness to attain liberation. We simply need to free attention's embeddedness in the conviction, the pretense of self.

In creating times of periodic solitude in our lives, we are creating a circumstance in which there is nowhere else to turn. In seclusion, we've blocked off the normal escape routes. There is no one to blame. There is no one to distract us, to influence us, to entertain us, or to prop us up.

In solitude we are left with the way it is for us. We're left to sit nakedly with self. It becomes very personal before it becomes very impersonal.

The ego has less traction in solitude. There's not much to work with. None of the usual suspects are present. With them absent, we can see one of the real culprits: attachment, that mental affliction present in every human mind. To free ourselves from attachment is to no longer grasp at a mental image of something we presume to be "out there" that, when added to the sense of self, we believe will make us whole and happy. We can begin to experience wholeness, already complete and sufficient. We become free of the tension of clinging to arisings, free to appreciate each new and fleeting arising each new and fleeting moment.

In many ways, we have spent a long time afraid to be alone with our own thoughts. We're reluctant to leave the fictional narrative upon which we've placed our fictional self. Our reluctance to go into solitude indicates that we already have a sense of what we've been hiding from, what we have wished to deny. Many of us have a vague sense of how precariously we skate on the thin ice of unexamined assumptions and a strong sense of fear as we contemplate a tumble to the depths. Our first impulse as we touch the edge of a paradigm is to quickly back away.

This reluctance to sit alone with ourselves in naked inquiry changes, to be sure, as we progress along the noble path. We come to cherish times of solitude, recognizing them as blessings and periods of rich nurturing, rich learning. Initially, though, we have reservations.

In many ways, we're afraid to look at, to stare down, the tangled and multilayered swarms in our minds, the swirls of "I" and "me," the congested energy on which we impute self. It takes some courage to face not only our thoughts and beliefs and assumptions but also our tensed identification with them. We've harbored them, with all of their accompanying emotions, for so long. We're afraid of what we might find in there, afraid of loosening the lid on the deep wells of sadness and remorse and disappointment, all of our stored hurts. We are afraid of our own fear.

We're afraid that the story that we've been telling ourselves all along about who we are and what our life has been about and why things are the way they are will be jarred and shaken. If we're not the story, the fabrication of a life's narrative, who are we? Until we have a deeper sense of being, ego is all we know. And we cling to it, we're attached to it, no matter how old we are, and no matter how ineffectual ego is.

Most of us have an immense reluctance to think that we might have been wrong all this time. Many of us have that habit pattern of wishing to be right more than we wish to be happy.

It takes solitude and silence—and all of the other special conditions of awakening—to recognize that the sense of "I" and "me" and "mine" is exactly the cause of all of our reactive stress and our sense of limitation. Much as the ego may have arisen as a defense, once spun into motion it dragged us, with great harm, along its unconscious way.

Our practice of freeing attention from ego doesn't have to be a dreaded chore. If we allow our intention to awaken to direct our lives as its central focus, every experience funnels toward the purpose. Laughing and lightness are allowed. In fact, our playfulness will return to us like a wandering puppy, if we've lost it.

Our playfulness will grow. There's a childlike quality in spiritual maturity. We can recapture much of the joy and wonder and innocence that were ours as a child. Those qualities just got cast to the side and deadened. They can be resurrected.

To cultivate and gather the causes and conditions of awakening doesn't mean that our life must have the reveille bell and drill sergeant of boot camp. Seeing what needs to be done, we simply do it. We recognize that we are the ones who benefit from staring down our own attachments, from taking a deep look at ourselves. It can be a joy and an adventure.

Initially, it takes attention and effort to incorporate circumstances that give rise to awakening in our lives. It's a bit like when we first learned to ride a bike. You push down on what pedal first? How can I balance and steer at the same time? How do I brake? Yikes. So much to remember. Then it all becomes second nature—then we can have the joy of racing downhill with the wind behind us or the quiet peace of cycling slowly through a palm hammock by a dark and lovely river.

It's important to see that it is only our ignorance, and the attachment born of ignorance, that wishes to turn away from what's happening, from what's going on inside us. We reside in illusion, in mistaken conception, when we believe that our suffering, as we experience it in the arising of habitual painful patterns, is so strong that we can't face it.

Without mindfulness, we wish to distract ourselves. Most of us have spent decades doing it. We're very good at it. Our habit is to keep turning away. Ignoring, we remain in ignorance.

Solitude, with its nowhere to turn and no one to turn to, demands our courage. It is an act of bravery to turn into these hidden corners and to remain open enough for long enough to witness the beliefs they hold. We allow the patterns that have always lurked in those hidden corners, like trolls, to begin to dissipate in that witnessing. But to override our initial, habitual inclination to turn away takes courage, strength of heart.

Those who live in cold parts of the world are familiar with that inclination to clench up, to tighten up, as we first walk out into freezing weather. That tightening just makes us colder. It takes a deeper understanding, and a bit of courageous resolve, to unhunch our shoulders, to relax a bit and open up into the frigid air. But if we do, we actually feel a bit warmer. We can employ the same dynamics when we approach our pain and fear—any difficult emotion. We need just the tiniest bit of deeper understanding and the tiniest bit of courage to relax the reactive contraction of "me."

IF WE WISH to awaken, to use this time of our lives for spiritually ripening, we need, at some point, to put our fictionalized self and its stories and explanations and habits into the fire until there's nothing left to burn. We don't do this all at once. We go through progressive waves of deeper opening and more subtle insight. We coax ourselves through each increasing relaxation of the contraction, each deeper release of all of the habits of self-grasping and self-cherishing. At the point where it would be possible to burn off the last of selfing, there's not that much selfing left to burn.

It is kind and wise to question ourselves, to inquire. What am I doing to protect myself from life? What do I believe about me? What do I believe about my ability to control? Who am I if I don't get what I want? Who am I if the objects of my attachment disappear? Who am I without the labels? Who am I without the stories, now decades old? Who am I without the explanations and justifications, so often repeated? Who am I without the habits? Who am I without the fears?

It is wise to look precisely at where we're afraid and at what we're afraid of. It's wise to look precisely at those things we might feel inadequate to handle. These are our hidden corners. And it is to our hidden corners that we typically relegate our fears and our perceived neediness.

In what circumstances would who I am now not be enough? What is the belief in my own inadequacy in facing down these fears? Where do I feel insufficient? That sense of insufficiency always arises in reactive relationship to our attachments, whether the attachment be to people, objects, or circumstances.

Breathing in, we fortify our courage. Breathing out, we release our fears.

Breathing in, we strengthen our intention. Breathing out, we open to the way it is.

Our work is in solitude. It's done with exquisite tenderness and profound openness. That tenderness and openness is based on our own growing confidence, the maturity of practice that allows us to remain increasingly nonjudgmental, to rest more frequently in the state of always-already-complete perfection.

The task is to arrive at the experience of trusting in our own sufficiency. We will never be able to feel sufficient or complete or confident as long as we continue to harbor our attachments, both examined and unexamined. We will always remain with the sense of insufficiency for as long as we allow our peace and stability to be contingent upon the satisfaction of our desires in what appears to be other than self.

Self always feels insufficient. In solitude, we can begin to heal our wounds of insufficiency.

Self always has the urge to grasp. We work with our attachments, remembering that all that can be lost will be lost. We remember that everything to which we are attached is our own mental image. We have grasped on to our mental images as if they existed independently of our own mind.

We've been shadow boxing, exhausting ourselves with inner isometrics. We've been trying for decades to rearrange and choreograph our own mental images. We can ask ourselves how well that has been working.

We will never feel sufficient or complete with a mind fractured into a thousand labels and fictions. There is no sense of wholeness when we allow our experience of life to be dominated by a tangled swarm of habit patterns that are often in conflict, like gulls greedily fighting over a fish. Diminishing and letting go of the hold of attachment, we can accomplish the spiritual task of feeling sufficient. We can transform loneliness into aloneness when we move beyond self.

In solitude, there is no need for our worldly persona. We can begin to witness our mental image of self as we imagine we appear to others. We can begin to see the mask as we wish others to see it. We can see how we've spent so long tweaking it from behind to achieve our desired goals, our desired reactions from others, our own reactions to our own self-image. We can begin to see it as the illusion it is. We can begin to see it as the prison it is. We can let go of our attachment to it, recognizing that it is incapable of orchestrating the happiness we seek.

Solitude allows for the gradual letting go of our images and our attachment to them. We begin to really see what attachment does to peace.

This gradual letting go doesn't proceed in any linear way or in any planned way, even for the most organized among us. It unfolds as it will unfold, upheld by intention. There are fields of golden glory and there are desolate and despairing wastelands. We just sit and witness and let go even when it is hard to sit and witness and let go—and we sit and witness and let go of the feeling that it is hard, too. If we fall back into unmindfulness, we refuel with intention and compassion and align ourselves in present-centered awareness, again and again and again.

Released into a greater sense of sufficiency, with greater freedom in the face of our own graspings, we can transform loneliness into aloneness. We can create the platform for continued ripening. We own our own practice. We own our own peace.

In taking our spiritual practice as a personal responsibility, we go deeply into self. It is another of the paradoxes of spiritual practice that the more deeply we go into self, with wise intention, the more awareness becomes free of self.

It's like the work involved in digging out after a blizzard, digging through the snow and clearing the downed trees and electric wires and stalled cars so that the road is clear. The digging out is the work we do to develop our capacity to discover our own essential nature.

As Ken Wilber puts it, "The more I go into I, the more I fall out of I." To go into I is to see through the illusion, to recognize the fiction and land, unobstructed, in beyond-self.

To INCORPORATE SOLITUDE in our lives in these years of our old age is to cultivate holy aloneness—void of all influences, a clear screen for witnessing our own habituated patterns. In solitude, we begin to see such patterns in stark clarity. Like all illusions, they dissolve upon investigation. Solitude allows us to see through many of the thoughts and assumptions of consensual reality. It allows deeper insight into the true nature of appearances.

Sufficient, alone, in solitude, with awareness moving beyond the self that we've clung to so personally and particularly, we allow maximum development of our absolute uniqueness. Without self-consciousness, our uniqueness can blossom. Freed from attachment to self, we simply are. This is nonreferential ease. The living being thrives in wisdom and a boundless heart. The functioning self remains not faceless but a wonderfully unique vehicle for spirit—the only one of its kind. Identity isn't lost; it's expanded. This is one of the gifts of the special condition of solitude.

SOLITUDE, PARADOXICALLY, can also bring us into deep connection. Opening into freedom, we allow opening into communion. That deep opening to communion, to interbeing, depends on freedom from attachment to self. The contraction of self cannot allow the experience of interconnection. It has no conceptual category for it. The contraction of self has always been based on the misconception of being separate.

We can, in solitude, have the deepest of realizations of interbeing. Our experience of being comes to be known not so much as a separate entity but as a process through which our intention, aligned in grace, steers us. In grace, we begin to live in connection. There arises an intense awareness of relationship, of all the small and interconnected miracles we never noticed in our rushed and busy lives.

Our own breath, breathed by seven billion other human beings, shared by immeasurable flora and fauna. Our own body, created from the same stuff as the stars. A vast organic process of existing, of being. Every arising conditioned by every other arising in each stunning moment that fills this hallowed cosmos. Without continuous, attached reference to self, we can rest our awareness in this interbeing, the awe-filled wonder of interconnectedness.

Thoreau came to know this on Walden Pond. John Muir, alone for so long in the majesty of Yosemite, came to see that "when we try to pick out anything by itself, we find it hitched to everything else in the universe."

The intense focus on exploring the self in solitude leads into awareness beyond self. Awareness beyond self allows our uniqueness to flourish. With the same sense of paradox—often defined as the way truth appears to our conceptual minds—our deliberate seclusion opens us into realization of our inextricable existence in the indivisible web of being.

FORGIVENESS

LIBERATION FROM AVERSIONS; FREEDOM FROM ANGER AND JUDGMENT

> Let what distracts you
> cease.
> Let what divides you
> cease.
> Let there come an end
> to what diminishes
> and demeans, and let depart
> all that keeps you
> in its cage.
>
> —Jan Richardson

Anger and judgment, of both self and other, are among the many ways in which the mind of aversion can arise. Many of us have trouble letting go of these mental afflictions. Our anger, with its reasons and blames, seems righteous. Similarly, we have tendencies to find our judgments justified and true; we have a tendency to harbor them and keep collecting evidence. We've all thought, at one point or another, that something or someone needs to be accountable for all of the unhappiness that we've endured.

Clinging to our misconceptions, we sometimes find it hard to forgive, both ourselves and others. Clinging to our misconceptions, we ordinarily don't stop to examine the real culprit—the mind of aversion, the mind at odds with what is.

Aversion has many forms: disappointment, frustration, irritation, impatience, anger, judging, animosity, fury, rage, animosity, annoyance, and hate, for instance. The number of words we have in our language to describe the nuances of aversion is an indication of how pervasive and out of control this mind is.

Aversion arises through inappropriate attention. We're like the princess and the pea. Searching for comfort, resisting pain or suffering in any form, we set ourselves up to achieve an impossible goal. We want birth without death, meeting without parting, gain without loss, pleasure without pain. We want the impossible.

When it is not to our liking, we resist reality. This resistance is friction. Sooner or later, we—certainly not reality—will feel the pain of that friction. Our aversion, based on misconception, traps us in suffering, large and small, gross and subtle.

With the mind of aversion, we zero in on one small moment or one small quality or one small circumstance that strikes against who we think we are and what we think we need. We zero in on the pea. We exaggerate the bad qualities of that person or that arising, creating a loathsome caricature, much as war propagandists do. Anger is a strong pattern that can feed on its own ruminations. This mind poisons us.

THE PRACTICE OF FORGIVENESS allows us to take a deep, close look at the mind of aversion. It is a kindness both to ourselves and others to begin to examine aversion's dynamics as they operate in our own being.

Unveiled partially, as we begin to look and continue to practice with mindfulness, the ignorance of aversion and all of its illusions can begin to decrease in both frequency and intensity. We become a bit less unsettled, a bit more at ease, a bit more difficult to ruffle.

Unveiled completely, the ignorance of aversion and all of its illusions can vanish, as shadows disappear in the light. Imagine what it would be like to have a mind in which anger as aversion never arose again. Imagine what peace would feel like. And yet we so often cling to aversion, stewing away in its poison, filling our body with its toxins and our mind with its ignorance.

It is our mind of aversion, our reluctance to let go of anger and judgment, our reluctance to forgive, that stands as one of the primary obstructions to peace—familial, global, outer, and inner.

When it comes our time to die, we will see that so much that had seemed important—until those last few weeks and days and hours of our lives—simply slips away. We will witness and experience a profound opening into what is essential, what really matters. Forgiveness arises naturally in that opening.

Forgiveness liberates us from some of the bonds that bind us. It releases us from much anger, from judgments, from grudges. Forgiveness frees us from the ignorance that believes that love and compassion are only to be offered to those who appear to deserve them. It releases us from the stinginess with which we dole out kindness and from the contracted defensiveness in which we often hold our sense of self.

As we enter the time of dying, slights and grudges and enmity, once held so tightly, simply vanish in a far more vast awareness.

They dissolve as our sense of self softens, as it becomes more porous.

This process of forgiveness at the end of life does not happen instantly, especially for those who are unfamiliar with working skillfully with their own aversions. Gradually, though, as those who are dying live with the stark awareness of their numbered days, old hurts and dislikes and animosities simply fade into the background. Their relevance is increasingly unimportant. At some point deep into the transformative process of dying, they couldn't matter less.

Much more powerful minds of aversions arise as we die—specifically, the penultimate aversion to the end of "me." This is a maelstrom of aversion, no matter how outwardly quiet the enduring of it may be. This is the mother of all aversions. And it tends to blow old petty grudges out of the water.

For those in the transformative process of nearing the end of life-in-form, the psychospiritual stage of chaos is, most often, a time of great anguish. It is filled with anger and denial and depression and despair. These are all variations of the mind of aversion, of resistance to what is.

GRADUALLY, at the very end of life-in-form, these mental afflictions begin to weaken in intensity and lessen in frequency. They dissipate in the growing weakness of terminal illness, unimaginable if we've never witnessed it. And they soften and dissipate as the separate sense of self is melted away in confrontation with the great power and radiance of the ground of being, keeping its promise of impermanence.

We delete our blame or animosity or aversion to people or things that no longer matter at all, as we lie dying. They're simply no longer on our screen. There are far more compelling experiences of surrender and transcendence that occupy attention.

Forgiveness is demanded in this situation. Indeed, forgiveness becomes a given, even if first offered begrudgingly. A mind unwilling to forgive cannot enter the fine and subtle spaces of surrender and transcendence; it is too dense in its tightness, too gross in its misunderstanding.

Forgiveness is a big deal. Forgiveness is a cleaned slate. Without it, we have no prayer of entering the peace of presence.

We can choose to bring the special condition of forgiveness practice into these last years of our time here. To deliberately practice forgiveness leads to our sweetening. It will release any trace of bitterness.

Forgiveness softens us, loosening our deeply ingrained habits of aversion. It relaxes our crystallized beliefs, our hardened stances, and our tense bodies. It allows liberation from much that we, out of ignorance, thought was important. Forgiveness frees us from stuck positions that hold us in limitation, hold us unfree, keep us from now. With forgiveness, energy that had been congested and caught in a painful mind releases into awareness.

THIS SPECIAL CONDITION of forgiveness as a deliberately cultivated state of mind, as an ongoing practice, is central to every valid wisdom tradition. Its liberative value could not be more clear or more valuable. Jesus taught it with his life.

Each time we engage in forgiveness, we are releasing our awareness into greater freedom. We free it from the mental affliction of aversion. There is no freedom in aversion. Aversion is a blind and robotic mind that reacts negatively when our experience is not what we wish. We can see aversion in an amoeba. The mind of aversion is that primitive, that unthinking, that unnuanced.

We react with aversion when we don't get what we want. We react with aversion when we feel forced to deal with anything we don't want. Our bandwidth for "acceptable" is fairly narrow, unless we cultivate greater equanimity in our spiritual practice.

We all tack pictures on our mental walls of the way things are supposed to be. They're usually lovely pictures, self-referential each and every one. We don't like it when the reality we're experiencing doesn't match our expectations, our perceived needs, our demands of the universe, often unarticulated but still operational.

Only some degree of contemplative, meditative practice leading to greater mindfulness will help us with the mind of anger. Without that mindfulness, we believe utterly in the story line we've created. We believe that someone or something has harmed or hurt or thwarted us.

Moral discipline and the growing wish to do no harm will help us curb aversion's angry outburst. Inwardly, though, without sufficient wisdom, that battle may still rage. Just below the surface and resurfacing at any reminder, we remain anywhere from mildly irritated to furious at those who we perceive to be blocking our wishes or not treating us as our self-image requires.

We throw inner tantrums, very similar to those of a two-year-old. We might recognize that we're much too long in the tooth to publicly kick our feet on the floor, whining and pouting and screaming, but, inwardly, our reptilian brain breathes fire. Our elephant brain refuses to forget.

We can get pretty trapped in the mind of aversion. It is an opportunistic mind. It arises, pops out of the crowd, at any halfway "appropriate" justification. The mind of aversion grabs at straws.

Anger, no matter how seemingly benign, no matter how disguised it might be in frustration or irritation or disappointment, is always in search of a target. Anger in search of a target is a fairly powerful and ingrained habit pattern, like a large and well-organized hurricane that gathers many other surrounding storm systems in its spin.

We look outside, to what appears external, searching for a target to blame. In truth, the mind of anger does seem to prefer to engage with others rather than faceless situations. It's easier, and sad to say, sometimes more enjoyable, to focus our displeasure or our wrath on another being. We have a tendency to actually like to be angry, to engage in blame and grudging.

We blame whoever we've chosen, whoever seems to fit into our belief systems as a villain, for "causing" our unpleasant reaction, the negative feeling tone. Our unpleasant reaction is actually our own habit pattern, honed over decades. We, often, without mindfulness, are glad to have it appear that someone is causing our upset. The anger can feed on the blame.

We know, as we get older each day, that we will be confronted almost inevitably with situations that we do not want. We will face debilitation and loss of strength and reflex and diminution of many of the capacities we have so taken for granted. We may face growing dependence on others, who may or may not wish to have that task.

If the litany of losses has not already begun for us, we know that we will begin to lose that which we want, that to which we are attached, that which has become entangled in our very identity. We will, in one way or another, have to part from every single last one of our loved ones. We will part from every possession, every tribute, every memory. We will have to part, even, from the old faithful friend, the body.

It is a kind and a wise thing to free our mind from aversion in all of its forms while we have the time to practice and cultivate equanimity. It is a kind and wise thing to practice forgiveness far before our time of dying demands that we forgive.

We can practice forgiveness for all those we hold responsible for our past grievances, so tended and remembered. We can ask, at least in the quiet of our own minds and the depth of our own hearts, for forgiveness from all those whom we have harmed. We can practice forgiveness for all of the ways we've harmed ourselves with judgment and nonacceptance.

Before we can talk about practicing forgiveness, though, we need to look at our resistances to forgiving.

WE'VE RUN THROUGH our grievances, over and over, so many times that we've developed deep neural pathways of dislike, each one holding a caricature of the face of the person we deem responsible for our upset.

Many of us do not like to let go of our grudges. They are the props upon which many of our stories are built. And our stories are the props upon which our fictional selves, to which we are so attached, are built.

To forgive, we need to have cultivated enough mindfulness to see through our stories. It is only with mindfulness that we are able to see our stories as the narrative fictions they are. These stories are the paradigms through which we experience life-in-form.

A paradigm scoops up selected facts, ignoring all that doesn't fit. Within our paradigms, each of us looks at the world through the lenses of our own viewpoints, like wearing sunglasses that block certain frequencies of light. We see what our mind creates. We see what our mind believes.

Although others may see our paradigms, we don't see our own. We're like Pigpen encircled in his dust cloud, walking through the enclosures of our known world in a congested sphere of thoughts and beliefs and their accompanying emotions. And we don't like it when the fictions of another's paradigm, the dust particles of their surrounding dust cloud, don't agree with our own.

Without mindfulness, we hold all the stories of the paradigm as more than mere opinion, more than mere viewpoint. We hold them as true. We invest our own imaginings with the power of our own believing.

Anger is always about a past moment, even if the moment was a nanosecond ago. Anger is always about a story, an airtight story that we hold with a hardened heart. We stubbornly entrench ourselves in the fiction of "wronged" me. The mind of anger is like a dog worrying a bone. It can't let go. It doesn't even want to let go. Our grudges keep us in the past. For how many years have we harbored some of them? For all that time, we've missed now.

It is a curious thing about the human mind in that it returns over and over to the memory of the incident seemingly responsible for our upset or anger. It seems to be a phenomenon left over from humanity's earliest history when survival depended on nursing a grudge and eliminating its seeming cause, whether that be the tribe in the next valley or a wooly mammoth. It can help ensure our seeming safety in form, but it is a vestigial obstruction to awakening into formless awareness.

Anger is a habit pattern that always arises out of ignorance. It arises out of blind survival needs and is a primitive and undeveloped mind. It has no benefit at this point in our evolution. The mind of aversion gives rise to days of stress and fuming and preoccupation, broken friendships, lost opportunities, and decades of familial conflict. The mind of anger keeps centuries of war going, the grandson of a dead grandfather killing the grandson of the killer. And so it continues and will continue.

Many of us find it difficult at times to forgive and we stay trapped in a toxic relationship with an aspect of our own mind, a caricature of the perpetrator. We resist forgiveness because the mind of aversion, the mind of anger, has a tendency to want to hurt those who we feel have hurt us. To look at any of the variations of aversion mindfully, we can see that one of the dynamics of the habit pattern is that it is so coiled and poised, so ready to lash out. The mind of anger is often hot and seething and jagged, so uncomfortable that it becomes like a pressure cooker needing to let off steam.

We resist forgiveness for many reasons. We may feel convinced that we're "right." We may have a tendency to feel that to forgive is to allow the strongly resisted notion that the other person might not be "wrong." We can self-righteously refuse to forgive so that it doesn't appear that we condone the other's actions.

We resist forgiveness because we are too caught up in, attached to, sometimes even relishing, the mind of aversion, unable to let go. We may want to withhold ourselves a bit more, keep that shoulder cold, in punishment. We may not want to forgive, thinking that forgiving the person we have constructed as our enemy might allow him or her to find benefit in our forgiveness. As long as we impute them as enemy, we begrudge them benefit.

Before forgiveness, we live in a dense, entangled, entrenched mind. A grudge wishes to harm. It has no generosity. Lack of forgiveness deepens our ignorance. Lack of forgiveness deepens our stress. The two, stress and ignorance, always go together.

Anger, grudges, lack of forgiveness cause nothing but harm. To closely examine the mind of anger, the unforgiving mind, is to see that it has no beneficial function. It is wise to do this examination of our own mind of aversion, to directly recognize its toxicity and develop the wish to be free of it. Any mind of aversion, any resistance to forgiveness, harms us.

Aversion, a negative reaction to what is, harms us physically, emotionally, interpersonally, and spiritually.

To hold a grudge keeps us chronically bathed in stress hormones, disrupting not only our peace of mind but also this precious and fragile body, intricately dependent upon optimum well-being.

Because attention can only hold one object of attention at a time, anger and happiness can't coexist. They're like Clark Kent and Superman. They're never seen together. They're mutually exclusive states of mind.

To live in an angry state of mind is to live without peace. At its extreme, we can't sleep, and enjoyment is out of the question. Even if we were to go to the most wonderful restaurant in town for a much-anticipated dinner, with anger we can't even enjoy the food.

The mind of anger harms relationships, often bloodying the people we love most. So often our regret for the words coming out of our mouth follows the words by only a microsecond. The mind of anger is king of the world in the moments when it's nurtured. It overrides every good intention, every inclination to kindness and compassion. Truly, it is one of our single most destructive emotions. Just in the last hundred years, tens of millions have died in the name of anger and aversion.

To harbor the mind of anger is immensely harmful to us in a spiritual sense. It prevents any positive growth we intend. It is an obstruction to awakening.

THE MIND of anger often appears as judgment. We can turn this judging against anyone for just about anything. Judging others, we shore up our own beliefs and assumptions. Judging others allows us to feel superior. That wish to feel superior is harmful. It feeds our fictional self, keeping us in ignorance. Judging others rips us out of interbeing and connection. It arises from ignorance and obstructs compassion.

Judgments also harm the people we judge, even if our judgments are never spoken aloud, even if our judgments are conducted in fleeting drive-bys—toward the slow driver who made us miss the light, toward the coughing lady with the screaming kid in the next seat on the plane. Judging puts out a directed negativity and adds to the toxicity of the world. It is on the same continuum as bullying, but more subtle and covert. Our judgments are a testimony to the slyness ego developed in keeping our mental bullying hidden.

At times, we turn the mind of judgment against ourselves. We have a tendency to condemn any aspect of our self that we deem to be unworthy or inadequate. We can trace this back to pure survival instinct. Those perceived qualities of our psyche judged to be unworthy or inadequate threaten our security, threaten the way our self-image wishes to be seen.

Self-judgment, self-hatred, self-loathing all plunge us into the realms of hell. What a painful and destructive narrative we write for ourselves with those minds. What a painful and destructive narrative we then believe. What an anguishing universe to create. We need to forgive ourselves as well.

Grudges and judgments and aversions all mire us more deeply in selfing. They entangle us in all the stress and unease and lack of peace that selfing gives rise to. We dig in deep, in the mind of anger, the mind of aversion, and create much suffering for ourselves.

IN A POWERFUL TEACHING, a man came up to Buddha and spit in his face. Ananda, Buddha's disciple, was shaken by this profound disrespect and took off to reprimand the spitting fellow. Buddha called Ananda back saying, "We have no way of knowing what ideas this man has about me. He wasn't spitting at me. He was spitting at his own notion."

It's a powerful message. This insight, "he was spitting at his own notion," can pierce through to the part of us that recognizes truth. But it can only pierce through if there's some porousness, some permeability in our paradigm. We have to have already softened and disassembled a bit of our defensive habit patterns, through intention and mindfulness, for that piercing to occur.

Every beam of insight needs to find a way through the defenses. The level of transformation effected by any insight is dependent upon the depth of access of the insight and its intensity. Insight can't penetrate hardened resistance, righteous in its own convictions. Softened, we can begin to apply the truth we are able to recognize and embody it throughout our each and every ordinary day.

We have to be willing to see through our narrative to the truth. We have to be willing to want peace. We say we do. Are we waiting for our family or our neighbors or our government to declare it? We have to ask ourselves, how deep and how earnest is my own intention for peace? Am I willing to be peaceful? Where am I not peaceful? Where are the inner battlegrounds? Am I willing to let go?

To FORGIVE is not to condone actions that are negative or harmful. With discriminating wisdom, compassion speaks against actions that can't be condoned. To forgive is not to allow one's self to continue to stay in harm's way. We can forgive and still get ourselves out of a situation that is unhealthy or intolerable, toxic in any way. Forgiveness speaks and acts with no intent to harm, but it can speak firmly and act decisively. Awakening is a practice of awakened action, an engaged practice of the heart, eventually embracing every moment, every situation, every living being.

Forgiveness is not about the act of another, as we've perceived it. We want to focus our attention on forgiveness itself, not on the act that appeared to give rise to the upset to begin with. Forgiveness, an inner reworking, an inner letting go, is necessary to free our minds. To attain the contentment and the peace we seek, we need to liberate ourselves from a stuck position. There is no growth possible in a stuck position. There is no freedom or innocent presence possible in a stuck position. Forgiveness is a release from our own anger.

It is helpful to practice the letting go that allows forgiveness. We can live each moment within the understanding of subtle impermanence, within the understanding that we are born anew in each moment. The actions that led to past grudges or the judgments that led to past condemnations do not exist in the present moment any more than the water at the precipice of a waterfall is the same water that was at the precipice a moment ago.

We can, deeply intentional within a quieted mind, sit with these contemplations and practice letting go into forgiveness. We can ask ourselves who we need to forgive and what is our resistance to doing so. We can look at how we judge ourselves and let go into forgiveness and release.

Forgiving, of both self and others, is a letting go. We let go of the past, of the story, of aversion, of stress and unease, of self. Awakening occurs through releasing.

Forgiving self is liberation from guilt. The weight and misdirection of selfing is detrimental enough, without adding another layer of ignorance with guilt. Guilt is a heavy cloak; it adds weight to our self-reference. The release from guilt frees attention and energy to be used in much more beneficial ways.

In this letting go, adopted as a special condition that catalyzes our awakening, we choose to open our attention to a more panoramic view. We let go of the tightness of our conviction. This allows deep insight into who we believe ourselves to be, what we think we need, in what situations we feel ourselves to be inadequate or vulnerable.

Forgiveness is a good practice to deliberately cultivate in our lives. We can witness our own stuckness, our resistance, and work to break out beyond the tight horizons of the fiction we've written by contemplating alternative accounts, more beneficial views. Choosing the most beneficial view is a sign of growing spiritual maturity. Looking for a more beneficial view, we can wiggle our story a little to the right, a little to the left, just like we'd wiggle a loose tooth for one of our kids.

Any object of anger is equally and more beneficially an object of compassion.

WE CAN BEGIN to see that, within our paradigm, our own minds are the source of both the caricature of the other and the animosity directed toward that caricature. When our awareness moves beyond the paradigm, the enmity and the emotional memory all fall apart like a house of cards.

Letting go of our story is a sudden insight, a clearing. It's like being on a stage set for a movie of the Old West and watching someone suddenly tear down the backdrop. Beyond the painting of cactus and high desert and blue sky, we can see the busy Hollywood lot behind the screen. Letting go of our story is that dramatic in terms of changing what we see. The object of our anger has always only been a mental image, a construction and an obstruction.

We can heal our own wounds when we stop blaming others for them. When we take aversion out of the mind, we can attend to the wound with wisdom and compassion. It's all more spacious and more workable when we free ourselves from our stories and the sense of self who took things so personally.

We can, if we choose, engage in a formal sitting practice periodically, looking for our remaining aversion, anger, judgment, and lack of forgiveness of any kind. We can deliberately soften and loosen and lighten each holding, letting go as fully as we can. We can think of this as purifying our minds. It is a powerful practice.

As we grow more adept at forgiving, more wise as to the benefits of forgiving, we can practice forgiveness in each present moment with no Dharma lag whatsoever. Once we have recognized the faults of lack of forgiveness and have come to see how to cultivate forgiveness, we might as well engage in forgiving immediately, cutting the whole drama that might have ensued off at the pass.

Instant processing. New water on the crest of the waterfall. No more keeping the past as a dusty veil obscuring the present.

Our sense of identity vastly expands when we let go of our aversions. We experience a greater freedom when we deliberately choose to release our investment in old and mistaken stories. Compassion can arise in us for every other human being who suffers passively when the destructive mind of aversion remains unconscious.

With the practice of forgiveness, the life lived becomes more harmonious. The awareness experienced rests in deeper and more stable equanimity. The wish to forgive, to never hold attention in lack of forgiveness, grows as we experience the benefits of letting go into forgiveness.

To adopt forgiveness as a periodic formal practice and to practice forgiveness with whatever is arising, moment-by-moment, in our ongoing daily lives is wise. To become adept at forgiving is skillful means.

To bring an open willingness to forgive to each moment is to create a future for ourselves and all others that has less strife and stress and far more generous compassion. It would be a gift to our suffering, torn, and conflicted world if we were to embody this mind of spacious equanimity as part of our commitment to spiritual ripening.

May we all develop our capacity to let go of the past, let go of animosity and aversion and judgment, let go of our congested and blinding paradigms, let go of attachment to the self. That attachment is the ultimate troublemaker. Forgiveness, the letting go of aversion, is the ultimate peacemaker.

As we age, may we all hold the space for peace in our world.

> For all the ways that I have harmed another in any way,
> either knowingly or unknowingly,
> through ignorance and confusion,
> I ask for forgiveness.
>
> For anyone who has harmed me in any way,
> either knowingly or unknowingly,

through ignorance and confusion,
I offer my forgiveness.

For all the ways that I have harmed myself,
either knowingly or unknowingly
through ignorance and confusion,
I heal these wounds with forgiveness.

—TRADITIONAL BUDDHIST PRAYER

HUMILITY

LIBERATION FROM PRIDE AND THE ILLUSIONS OF PERFECTIONISM; RELEASE INTO ORDINARINESS

> It is almost impossible
> to overestimate the value of true humility
> and its power in the spiritual life.
> For the beginning of humility is the beginning of blessedness
> and the consummation of humility is the perfection of all joy. . . .
> In perfect humility all selfishness disappears.
>
> —THOMAS MERTON

FOR THE DYING, humility arises naturally.

It is humbling to be the one who needs to accept assistance with sipping water, with using the toilet, even with raising our head. It is humbling to be at the mercy of the medical staff for whom we are only one of many patients and upon whose kindness we depend—for medication and treatment and gentleness in all of the ways in which they prod and poke us. It is humbling to have others bathe our bodies and trim our nails and wipe our bottoms.

We learn humility, choicelessly, as we die. We can present a physical appearance that can be frightening. The effect of disease on a body is a rough visual; people often back away, even if only inwardly.

It is humbling to have others around us in our most intimate moments of enduring pain and fear, in the unbelievably profound intimacy—far more intimate than lovemaking—of active dying.

It is humbling to receive the love that pours out for us at the end of our life. It is humbling to recognize that we are helpless to thwart the mortal span life allots our appearance.

It is humbling to be an ordinary human being dying.

AGING CARRIES with it its own ample supply of opportunities to open to humility. It brings indignities. These are indignities in the normal sense of the word, the conventional view of what's "dignified," established in a worldview that posits midlife as the exemplar of an adult human life.

It is humbling to be an ordinary human being living *and* aging.

Ordinary tasks become harder. Seeing well enough to drive at night becomes out of the question. Trying to count the change at checkout, while the impatient crowd, plastic in hand, waits behind us, can be humbling. Family gatherings, except for the curious few of the younger ones who want to hear about our years, are occasions where the action clearly is elsewhere. All of the younger ones—and they're all younger—are in the busy-ness of their lives. Often, they are engaged in interests that no longer hold much attraction for us, just as we, with our thoughts and silent, unshared memories, hold little interest for them.

The hours in doctors' waiting rooms, surrounded by other aging beings who also spend hours of their time in the same waiting rooms, are humbling. Condescending advertisements on television direct us to try their new reverse mortgage that comes with a free magnifying glass. It's humbling to be viewed as easy prey.

A friend told me of a dream in which she was a wispy-haired, big-eared, big-nosed, toothless elderly woman lying on a gurney. In the dream, she was in an emergency room, clearly in crisis, with two young male doctors bent over her in concern. A gorgeous young woman passed by, walking down the hall. The dreaming friend watched and felt the two doctors' attention slip away from her and become riveted on every step the pretty young girl took as she walked her way past their view. The friend bolted right up from her deathbed, where a moment before she was barely breathing and unable to lift even a finger, and, in a strong and indignant voice, said to the two doctors, "I was pretty once, too!"

The view in the mirror is humbling, with its sags and wrinkles and funny brown age spots and veins that seem to stick out a lot more than they used to. The young cannot imagine us young any more than they can imagine themselves old. And we cannot believe this old face and this old body. And, yet, even unrecognizable, we continue to impute "I" upon it.

As WE NOTICE ourselves shrinking away from these visible and experiential evidences of our aging and of our growing irrelevance in a youth-oriented culture, we can use the very shrinking away to highlight the places where pride still lurks in us.

To whatever degree we still have pride—the love of self-aggrandizement, the love of feeling superior or special—it's time we take a look. To release ourselves from pride far before death comes to find us, to find the liberation into humility far before death, enables us to live in grace in the midst of life.

Pride is arrogant. It can be distinguished from the healthy joy and fulfillment that we can feel in accomplishment. That healthy joy and fulfillment wants to be shared. Pride shares with no one. It is a stingy mind, wanting recognition only for itself.

With wisdom, pride is seen as a mind that is vulnerable to the eight worldly concerns that trap us—concerns of loss and gain, pleasure and pain, fame and shame, praise and blame. These concerns or conditions exist as magnets for our unexamined habits of mind in every moment. Attachment and aversion are likely to arise in each of these eight circumstances and pride is quick to follow. As always, our attention is caught and entrapped whenever the energy of self and the energy level of old habit patterns are higher than the energy of our mindfulness.

The mind of pride is a place where the unfolding of our awakening process can get snagged, a place where we create suffering for both ourselves and others. Pride is a dangerous quagmire if we wish to avoid continued suffering in the same old unmanaged habits, particularly the unmanaged habit of selfing.

If we are truthful with ourselves, most of us would have to admit that most of the time we truly, deeply, spontaneously cherish only ourselves or those we hold as "mine," even after we've practiced on the path for a while.

With this mind of self-cherishing, we filter experience. We pick and choose only the snapshots of our imaginings that suit our purposes at the time. In the mind of pride, we believe in and exaggerate our estimable qualities and possessions, wish them to be recognized, and seek to feel special. We entangle ourselves in the sense of self, which is to say in tension and limitation, when the mind of pride holds sway.

The mind of pride can manifest in several ways. With pride as vanity, we think, "My ego is better than your ego." Upon closer examination, the thought is more like "the mental image I hold of myself is superior to the mental image I hold of the mental image I think you hold of yourself." With pride manifesting as unworthiness, a false humility, the ego remains just as entrenched as when pride manifests as arrogance. Both states of mind—pride and its mirror image of inferiority or unworthiness—are fixed in self-absorption. They both cling in attachment to an imputed self, regardless of the value or worth seen in it.

Self is a familiar comfort zone, even when it is permeated with the judgment of "unworthy." Thomas Merton saw deeply into this dynamic when he said, "Perhaps I would rather be guilty and weak in myself than strong in Him whom I cannot understand." Tara Brach, a respected Dharma teacher, refers to this as "the trance of unworthiness."

PRIDE, LIKE GUILT, adds another layer to the already painful weight and congestion of selfing. It makes our life and our awakening more difficult.

It is painful to be around someone else's pride. Unless we've done some work on this mind of pride in ourselves and have developed some nonreactive equanimity with it, we get hooked on another's pride. Hooked, either rivalry or feelings of hurt and inferiority arise. Snags everywhere.

How painful it is to be prideful ourselves. The rush we get from parading our pride is a fabricated high, an inflation opportunity for the ego. With any cultivation of mindfulness, we can feel how the popping out of our pride lowers whatever contentedness or peace we had the moment before pride arose. Think of the effort involved in the wish to be recognized as superior, as special. What squandering of energy and time, attention and opportunity. Time is ticking away and we're too old for this.

The mind of pride is an adventitious feeder. It is an omnivore. It's always popping in, whenever it can. In can pop in as quickly as a finger snap, sometimes even in our deep meditative and contemplative experiences. If we allow pride to sidetrack us, it utterly tailspins us out of any moment of insight or transformative potential.

Pride keeps us trapped in the mental image we're working, hard and constantly, on presenting to the world and certainly attempting, with the stress of denial, to present to ourselves. Pride keeps us separate from others. Our need to stand out, or to be better than, rips apart connection, utterly precludes mutual respect.

Pride keeps us fragmented in an interior way, also. The mind of pride suppresses all aspects of the psyche that don't fit into our chosen persona. Our persona is a defense strategy. It can't allow any flaws in the presentation. We want the make-up right and the hair brushed just so before we let the cameras roll.

Pride creates a rift in our own being between our mental images of the parts we want seen, the parts we're happy to own—our persona, and our shadow—our mental images of the parts we wish to hide, the parts we haven't yet healed and owned and accepted. Pride is a fragmented mind with its own strong agenda. It is always at odds with itself, in tense isometrics. It leaves us conflicted, like a congress paralyzed in blind and deep partisanship.

Attachment to the sense of self limits our access to the boundlessness of our potential. Pride adds an entangled, congested extra layer of limitation, of obstruction. It keeps us more bound in smallness and pettiness and the inessential, by orders of magnitude.

In this fragmented state, self-acceptance and the peace of self-acceptance become impossible. We consign ourselves to live at the furthest reaches from our center, at the very periphery where we imagine our mask interacts with our mental images of others.

Superiority and arrogance, the deep need to be recognized, are the overt manifestions of pride. Perfectionism is pride's appearance in more covert form: "I'm not going to expect perfection from other people, but I have higher standards for myself."

We can follow the thread of perfectionism's imperative down almost to a sense of life and death. For most of us who have any kind of perfectionist mentality, we will probably find, when we begin to poke apart the belief and examine it with some clarity, that it stems from some emotionally laden assumption made early in childhood: "If I am not perfect, I won't be loved, I'll be rejected, I'll be punished," and, even the worst thing a child can think of, "I will die."

Fear and attachment keep perfectionism alive; fear and attachment fuel it. Again, we allow ourselves to follow the counsel of a six-year-old. If our intention remains clear about using these last years of our life to spiritually ripen, it is a good thing to examine what perfectionism we have left to weed and eventually uproot.

Perfectionism is an obstacle. We can't productively engage in a noble practice with perfectionism. We can't wake up into awareness beyond self when our strongest intention is to perfect the self.

We can use this time to begin to deliberately replace whatever habits of perfectionism that might remain with a far more clear and realistic commitment to integrity. Rather than bringing perfectionism into the spiritual path, an impossibility from inception, we can focus on bringing commitment to sincerity, commitment to intention.

Commitment comes from the heart's longing. It is qualitatively different from striving for success.

In any of the manifestations of the mind of pride, we are so far from the divine, from spirit. Pride is a lonely and alienating mind, utterly dependent upon the appropriate nods and words and signs and indications of our sought recognition. Pride has nothing to do with the radiant and holy, unselfconscious awareness that is our essential nature. It is a huge obstruction to that awareness. Mired in form, as it is, it can never mix with the formless.

BEFORE WE CAN let go of perfectionism and pride—as well as its equally weighted polar opposite, unworthiness—we need to see how these minds arise in us. We want to heal the wounds that give rise to them. Pride keeps us from transforming many of the mental habits that are the cause of our tensions, gross and subtle. It ties us to a fixed and stuck position, far from nonreferential ease.

We will always be pulled back to the unhealed wounds that the mind of pride tries to ignore. To keep the ego puffed is to cover up the woundedness that the judging self calls inadequacy. Arrogance is the large front of a large back of insecurity.

Part of our practice, if we choose to designate these last years as an awakening retreat, can include a commitment to explore where we are caught in pride. Sitting in the determination to look, we can begin by noting all of the aspects of aging that stab our pride, that touch a sore point.

Does it bother me to be ignored? To no longer be found desirable and attractive or powerful and strong? To no longer be found relevant? Does it bother me to be treated condescendingly or with deference? Does it bother me to be a geezer?

The little stabs, the little sore points, can highlight for us the fields in which we need to work.

As we sit in meditation with our pride, we can, in fairly short order, come to see that, in the mind of pride, ultimately we're making fools of ourselves. It's an absurdity to believe that my fictionalized self is better than your fictionalized self. We've been walking around in the emperor's new clothes, adorned in an inflated arrogance about a self that doesn't even exist in the way we conceive of it.

In the emperor's clothes, we're unable to admit to our own woundedness. No matter how much we practice and how much we grow in meditative experience, unattended wounds remain our bottom line. They need to be healed if we are to awaken. The very woundedness will keep pulling us back to attend to what is unhealed.

When we can begin to see the absurdity of our pride and set it aside, refusing to engage in it, we clear away the space to look at all of the wounds that pride and bravado attempted to cover up.

We have to acknowledge that we have wounds. Every habit pattern arose from a perceived wound. They hold us back like gaping holes in a foundation that can hold no stable growth, that needs attending.

It takes incredible humility to acknowledge our wounds and sit with them and treat ourselves tenderly. This humility is the beginning of our release into the great freedom of ordinariness. I, as has every other human being, have been wounded.

OUR PRIDE MAY fear the word *humility*. Our pride may recoil at the word *ordinary*.

There is a vast difference between humiliation and humility. Humiliation is weighted with shame, a hot, deep contraction of being, the sense of self so strong it wishes for nonexistence. We feel humiliation when our shame is exposed.

Humility has no shame. Humility is the release of the energy of stressful posturing, energy freed from self-reference. It is a release into the ordinary, light and spacious. It is freedom from the pressure of trying to be extraordinary. Ordinary is what we are. Ordinary is boundless.

Spiritual practice, as is dying, is humbling. It is humbling to witness our own patterns and our own destructive emotions.

That opening into humility is the journey and the goal.

WE NEED TO stop and sit and do some healing. We don't need to feel embarrassed that here we are at this age and we still have these old wounds, as many people our age do. We can think, "Thank goodness, I finally am taking the opportunity to heal them. Thank goodness, I have the opportunity to live my remaining time healed. Thank goodness, I have the opportunity to die healed."

Most of us have been like wounded deer running through the woods. We just kept running wounded for decades, pushing ourselves in spite of the wounds, maybe even running unaware of the wounds. We need to find the equivalent of a soft bed of long, green grass and give the wounds the time, attention, and compassion they require. We need to give our wounds, as we would with any beloved's wounds, meticulous attention, loving attention, healing attention.

In this healing state of mind, we can begin to see our ego as the sum total of all of our wounds and the ways in which we've become familiar with defending against more. When we go deeper into every habit pattern, we can see that it arose from a wound.

The ego is not so much evil—although it often engages us in acts that lead to harm, our own and others—as it is blind, unwise, misinformed, and misdirected.

Ego is like an oversensitive smoke alarm, part of our survival mechanism on overdrive. Even far along the path, after we've achieved some measure of freedom from attachment to the sense of self, we can still witness our habitual patterns gone a bit awry, feeling a bit threatened or needy, and giving bad direction. These energies can be wasteful or destructive.

To awaken, even to live more harmoniously, we need to harness these energies and manage them wisely.

SITTING, HEALING, in humility, we can begin to develop more compassion for the pain that begat ego and its habit patterns. With this compassion, we can use wisdom and wise intention to manage the ignorance of ego's impulses.

We want to retrain our hearts and minds. We want to retrain our brains and prune out all of their self-referential routes. We can redirect all of the neural loops that have habitually gone back to the primitive, blindly reactive brain. We can, with practice and deliberate self-compassion, transform the circuitry, heal the fractures of our being that were created in ignorance, and leave ourselves more integrated and synchronized, in greater harmony in our brain and in our being.

Practicing in this way is like taking an abused dog into our care and working with it. Treating the dog tenderly and lovingly, we can teach it new ways. This is the journey of our later years if we so choose: training in becoming a healed and functioning self through which the light of spirit can shine. This both demands and gives rise to the basic sanity of humility.

We can incorporate a rhythmic practice, if we wish, of sitting with our own woundedness. That woundedness wants to be embraced as much as the abused dog would. Our meditative, contemplative practice will undoubtedly, in due time, and maybe even rapidly, bring up the wounds that need our tender attention.

When these wounds arise, we simply sit in openness, in humility, in compassion. We sit with courage, with the purity of a parent's love for a beloved child. We allow pain to be present. It will come to the surface, like old shrapnel working its way out, if we allow it. We entrust the pain of the wounds to the loving care of whatever wisdom and compassion we have cultivated through our practice, the wisdom and compassion of formless awareness to which we have already opened.

Our unhealed wounds are multilayered, and their old and foundational roots pervade all aspects of our being. Below those unhealed wounds, at an even deeper level, is the wound of self, torn from the ground of being. It festers with the fear of death, the end of "me." Our deliberate healing will engender the courage and wisdom needed to let go of the self that fears death. With that release, the self melts back into the love from which it had imagined itself separate.

It is wise to sit periodically for the explicit purpose of healing, of practicing compassion and lovingkindness for ourselves. Eventually we may come to hold ourselves always in the embrace of this stance until there are no more wounds left to heal. We can let our heart break open in such humility that no new wounds arise.

When we're engaged in doing this healing work, initially we may notice that, over and over, the story upon which we have always relied to explain the wound wants to assert itself in our minds. It is best to skip the story. Occasionally we may use the story to evoke the feeling of an old wound, but once the feeling is generated, for the sake of simply healing the wound, we can let the story go, let it simply dissolve in our mind's eye.

Staying with the story just enmeshes us more deeply in our misconceptions. Although the story of the wound is a fiction, the pain is suffering. We want to attend to the pain, open to it, so that it can heal. We want to be like the mother who lovingly wakes her child from the grip of a nightmare.

Although there is no independent, inherently existent self, no "owner" of the suffering, we need to heal our wounds before we can, in deep and direct realization, release our attachment to the sense of self.

We want to maintain a delicate balance, a middle way, when we are working with wounds. We don't want to follow any advice to keep a stiff upper lip and repress the fact that we're wounded, nor do we want to follow advice that would keep us trapped in our identity as the walking wounded. We want to heal self without feeding self.

We do this with unconditional friendship and acceptance toward self, in humility. We do this with respect for the nobility of the practice, respect for the nobility of an ordinary human being taking the steps toward awakening. We keep a noble posture out of respect for our own potential, our own Divine Indwelling, our own buddhaseed.

It takes great humility to sit and allow the process of spiritual ripening to occur once we have gathered the necessary causes and conditions. The practice of deliberate, loving healing both requires and fosters humility, the end of pride.

WE MAY HAVE THOUGHT of the spiritual path as all-glorious, like a rosy-tinged, many-petaled lotus opening into unimaginable radiance. Maybe that's so, but the self will not be around to experience it, and there will be a lot of bugs and spiders and slugs that will scurry out of their hiding places in the lotus petals before those petals are fully opened and attachment to self overcome.

The spiritual path is not an airlift out of suffering. It is a journey of exploring the dynamics of our own interference with the experience of the ground of being. We inquire into our interference so that our interference might cease. Some passages of the journey include many long and sometimes discouraging experiences of realizing how lost we've been, in ways that perhaps we never allowed ourselves to feel before. Although it leads to greater and greater ease, the spiritual path is not all easy. It is, however, doable by any of us ordinary human beings, with wise effort and clear intention.

The spiritual path is work. If we are committed to awakening in these older years of ours, we need to organize our lives around this intention, in order to persist in the work and endure steadfastly in the hard passages. There are desolate stretches at the mercy of the powerful habits that are being resisted. There certainly can be dark nights and days—and much longer—of the soul.

These dark times open eventually into the simple experience of woundedness. Stripped of stories, even "spiritual" stories, they have emotional and physical components that we simply open to lovingly and allow ourselves to feel. No emotion is going to kill us. Every physical sensation is impersonal. We can breathe our way through the healing of our own wounds.

There are great releases of sorrow as we touch and heal wounds that have never been tended before. Sorrow is an interesting emotion. It can leave us feeling rain-washed. The tears we cry cathartically actually differ in their chemical composition from the tears we cry when our eyes are irritated. The tears of sorrow carry away more toxins. They clean us. They heal us.

Think of any cut we've ever had. It's remarkable: we're healable.

Healing is humbling work. Healing demands honesty, and honesty demands humility.

To commit to awakening is responsible and noble and it has dignity. It yields contentment. Our own commitment to wake up generates a boundless heart, benefiting everything and everyone. Released from pride, with humility and the freedom of ordinariness, we can help heal the world.

We begin healing the wounds in our own sense of self. We need a healthy, sound self to move awareness beyond self.

AFTER HEALING the wounds of this lifetime, the wounds of the story of this lifetime, we can turn to healing the four fractures that keep us locked in the fiction of self. In constructing this sense of self, we posited four dualities. These dualities, to the degree that they remain in us as unexamined convictions, remain as four falsehoods in all of our paradigms, the swirling congestions of views and reactions in which we live.

We drew four boundaries in the creation of a sense of separate self. They only dissolve when they are clearly seen for the conceptual fictions they are. The boundary lines we've drawn, and have continued to defend with stress and tension, are the boundary between shadow and persona, the boundary between body and mind, the boundary between life and death, and the boundary between self and all else.

The boundary lines of the four dualities are healed progressively as we die. That progressive healing increasingly releases the attention of the dying person into formlessness, the radiant ground of being that has informed every moment all along, always waiting for us. There is great joy as attention is released into awareness, returned home.

We've imagined the fractures of the four boundaries. We can heal the habitual patterns that have developed around the imagined fractures with our practice and our intention while still in the midst of life.

When we heal the wounds of the self, we own the self. We become whole. We become authentic. We dissolve the boundary between shadow and persona. Our intention to look and explore and lovingly and humbly attend to the wounds underlying our habit patterns releases us from pride. There is a liberation of the attention that had been held bound in a tense and often troubled persona. This energy releases into a healthy and refreshing humility, deep self-acceptance, and the freedom of ordinariness.

The boundary between body and mind is dissolved in deep and sustained meditative practice. Through focus on the rising and falling of the breath, mindfulness of breath, we bring our awareness out of the conceptual mind. Holding awareness in stillness, we can begin to recognize directly the insubstantiality, the wondrous yet still merely imputational quality, of both mind and body. We can recognize and experience that they are of one taste, forms churned from formlessness.

The boundary between life and death is dissolved as we steadfastly maintain our commitment to our meditative practice. We begin to have moments, increasing in both intensity and frequency, eventually to become stable, of recognition that attention can be freed from attachment to the self. When that attachment is released, the boundary heals. Beyond self, awareness simply is. It is outside of time, outside of temporality and finitude and mortality. Beyond self is our home. Dead or alive.

The boundary between self and all else is dissolved as we begin to live in awakened mind. Actually, the moment the boundary dissolves, awakened mind dawns. Duality dissolves. We dance the endless dance of form and formlessness's interbeing without self-reference. There is no difference between this mountain and that mountain, only momentary perspective. There is no difference between this congestion of energy and that congestion of energy, only momentary perspective. The same awareness shines through it all and our awareness rests, past self, in this recognition, in this nondwelling, formless, and holy space. This is awakening, enlightenment, illumination.

EACH OF US who chooses to awaken in these last years will undertake this journey in his or her own way, following the beneficial fabrications (anything in words is a fabrication, an approximation of truth) and instructions of whatever wisdom traditions resonate the most deeply with our own being.

All of this is undertaken not to attain enlightenment as some rainbow-haloed sainthood, our pride's fifteen minutes of fame. We have idealized mental caricatures of enlightenment until we go more deeply into the journey. For many people, enlightenment is seen as something for others more worthy. Many people hold enlightenment as something unattainable for all of us ordinary beings, although it's only beings who know themselves to be ordinary who can attain it. For some people, enlightenment can be seen as a bit boring. Life without drama sounds a bit too ho-hum. It holds no interest for them.

Awakening, though, is nothing other than liberation from suffering, from stress and unease and the limitation of contraction. That is the fundamental wish in all of us. That is what we all have in common: the wish to be happy and the wish to be free from suffering.

If we follow this path with a deep commitment to spiritual ripening, spiritual maturity, we will increasingly experience awareness freed from attachment to self and, thus, from suffering. Liberated, experiencing interbeing in the spaciousness produced by humility, we hold the wish for all others to be happy, for all others to be free from suffering.

We can stand as witnesses that this is an achievable goal. In doing so, we stand in divine pride. I bow to the Buddha, the Divine Indwelling, the radiant ground of being, in me. I bow to the Buddha, the Divine Indwelling, the radiant ground of being, in you.

Divine pride is grateful ownership. We own the nobility of our own essential being, but we own it gratefully. That gratitude prevents false pride from sneaking in. We can practice grateful ownership with any of our gifts. Our worth has always been present in our essential nature. If it has been obscured by unworthiness, divine pride is the manifestation of our changed relationship with our own essential nature.

We can hold any of the noble qualities that bring us to the heart of things—love, wisdom, compassion, generosity, humility—in divine pride. All of these noble qualities, available instantly the moment obstructions are removed, rest in the quiet zero point, the intersection of form and formlessness. To bring our heart and our mind to any of the noble qualities requires simply remembering them, bringing our attention into their frequency or energy level, and entering into the still point of present-centered awareness.

HUMILITY BRINGS a release into freedom, a profound and exhilarating release into ordinariness. No longer comparing and judging, we experience an incredible gain in the energy and ease that has been tied up for so long with posturing. This has nothing to do with obliterating the self but with transforming and releasing our attachment to the fabrication of self. We become more spacious, more simple. We become contented, living lightly. We become less caught in the congestion.

Empty of attachment to the self and the delusion of pride, which tightens that attachment even further, we create the newly freed room in our own spaciousness for others to also enter into awareness beyond the tight congestion of self. We become like a clearing in the woods or a lull in the storm, a quiet and open space that attracts others into it and offers them the opportunity to also find their bearings and adjust their compass toward home.

There is a great rush of freedom as we enter humility. Wisdom allowed the entrance and compassion naturally accompanies it. In humility, with wisdom and compassion, we make a more spacious world, where the experience of our communion and connection has fewer barriers and becomes more possible.

We can, if we wish, bear witness to the potential each of us has and the particular meaningfulness of this time of aging in a human life. Out of humility arises dignity. This is noble work.

To the decades of old age, a time filled with all that the worldly view holds as indignities, we can bear witness to the dignity of the wise use of this time. We can bear witness to dignity for ourselves and for all who will follow us. We can hold dignity with the humility of grateful ownership.

PRESENCE

LIBERATION FROM FRIVOLITY AND OTHER INESSENTIALS

> Stand still. The trees ahead and bushes beside you
> Are not lost. Wherever you are is called Here.
> The forest knows
> Where you are. You must let it find you.
>
> —David Wagoner

If we look even a tiny bit below the surface of our robotic habits of body, speech, and mind, most of us would have to admit that we feel lost much of the time. It is precisely that feeling of "lost" that the ego with its strategies tries to cover up, tries to Band-Aid and suppress. Most of us are so rarely *here*. Our attention is so rarely at home in *now*.

And, yet, here and now, in our depths—in intimacy, vulnerability, presence—is where we find the grace we long for. We already, on some level, know this. The yearning has always been awaiting our cultivation. The more we regain our capacity to be present—we all enjoyed it once—the more the majestic process of awakening can unfold with the ease of a longing that has always been here and a direction that has always been known. All that has ever separated our longing from that for which we long is the merest veil of misunderstanding.

There is no refuge outside of here and now, no stability, no reliability. Leaves in the wind, we have spent a long time lost in confusion. Most of us have spent a long time with our attention trapped in illusions, in frivolity, in the inessential, in the past and in the future. And we have paid a great price for this.

We have, so often, frittered away our own inexpressible potential through simply not knowing of it, not having explored it, having remained in ignorance of it. What if we were to draw a pie chart of where our attention and intention and concern have dwelled in our lives to date, all those irredeemable years? Would we want to take that piercing, graphic look?

There are so many experiences heading our way as we age, occasions when great anguish and strong fear and profound confusion could overtake us. The challenges we face could leave us feeling lost and whirling in a vast indifferent universe, were we not mindful. Even with greater mindfulness, anguish and confusion and other difficult emotions may well be part of what we meet.

Now is a good time to ask ourselves some piercing questions, to get a sense of where we are in our openness and our capacity for presence.

To effect transformation requires our maturity and commitment to our own deepest intention, as well as mindful vigilance. How sad it would be to lie dying with the same old unexamined habits claiming jurisdiction, still obstructing the beauty of our essential nature, still filling the space we occupy with ignorance and less than all we are. At that moment, we cannot beg for an extra day or an extra hour.

Imagine what it would be like to simply be present with the mystery and the immensity and the glorious, shimmering impermanence of this experience of life. Imagine what it would be like to live with a courageous heart, to not turn away, to stay open to what is difficult to face.

The vigilance required to ripen spiritually isn't that of a vigilante, like the self-righteous and merciless enforcers of tight paradigms in so many fundamentalist settings—including the fundamentalist settings in our own minds. Jack Kornfield, a deeply respected American Buddhist teacher, suggests instead that we hold mindfulness of moment-by-moment arisings with the vigilant stance of a mother with her baby. There is in the stance of that mother, in this meaning of *vigilance*, a sense of holding vigil—a deep respect, a moment-by-moment loving attentiveness, an awed wonder. There is, in holding vigil, a sense of quiet and compassionate and appropriate responsiveness.

The mind of vigil is a mind that is powerful enough to hold the deep stabs of the losses and diminishments of aging. With this mind, we can manage to stay present in, not turn away from, the painful experiences we may face. With this mind, we can manage to simply, stably, sanely be with the suffering that may be ours or our loved ones' without closing down or without getting lost in it. This present-centered awareness is the mind that will allow us to hold loving vigil through all of the times of grief that may lie in our future, all those moments that may pull up past, unresolved grief, as a magnet pulls up nails.

Mindfulness can help us stay present in each moment, radically accepting what our blind habits would have us flee. In the refuge of present-centered awareness, we can access the courage to remain with whatever is unfolding without losing our mindfulness. Present and mindful, there is less selfing. Presence has no room for self. Present, we need not feel lost and overwhelmed, as we do within the powerful undertows of selfing's reactions. We need not feel so afraid of getting swept away in the waves of reactivity that would wash us into the great ocean of suffering.

WHERE WE PLACE our attention literally creates the world in which we live and our experience of existence. Lost in pain, we live in a universe of suffering. Witnessing pain, we live in a universe permeated by compassion.

Learning to control the placement of our attention—learning mental pliancy—could not be more valuable if we wish to ripen into spiritual maturity, facing the challenges that await us and offering, from that maturity, the refuge of a boundless heart to ourselves and to the world. Such a skill is like getting the keys to the kingdom. Every wisdom tradition, recognizing the importance of trained attention, has chosen objects of meditation, chosen objects of focus, upon which to place and maintain placement of attention. This training in mental pliancy and attentional stability is recognized by many paths as a necessity for awakening.

These anchors for our attention, for the placement of our awareness, are countless. They replace our ordinary anchors of conception and sensation. The Buddhist tradition lists hundreds. In Christianity, such objects include the Jesus Prayer, the chosen word of Centering prayer, the generated mental states of love, adoration, and devotion. The practice of Advaita Vedanta remains in the constant inquiry "Who am I?" and the constant answer "I am." Jewish mystical practices emphasize *hashkatah*, mind quieting, and cultivating awareness of ever-present holiness. There are many pathways home and many methods to tame the wandering attention of unguarded habit patterns, all too eager to fire away in their familiar paths.

To engage in awakening, we need a stake to rope the monkey mind. Any chosen stake will do—the breath, a word, light, sound.

For those who are in the endstages of a disease process and nearing the experience called active dying, the special condition, transformative condition, of presence arises in the moment-by-moment focus on the breath. Breath as anchor. Breath as stake. Breath as keel and rudder and sail. When we are down to our last breaths, our attention is far less likely to wander haphazardly. How many of the finite number of breaths that I will breathe in this lifetime remain to me? This next inbreath. Will it come? This next outbreath. Is it the last? We are very present in such moments. There is no frivolity. Nothing inessential sweeps us back into dull and clouded mindlessness.

We develop the capacity to be present, the avenue into awakening, by practicing presence. Our capacity begins with intention and with the practice of mindfully and deliberately showing up in the moments of our lives.

We can, ordinarily, show up in the present for brief moments. The first outer bands of a tropical storm; a dolphin unexpectedly jumping from a wave; an intimate exchange with a friend or a pet or a stranger or a spouse; the touch of a grandchild's warm, new head. We can, with some earnestly intentioned practice, actually begin to show up, fully present, with a bit of increasing frequency and intensity.

For most of us who are making our way along the noble path, showing up is most likely to happen during formal sitting practice. We want to encourage and allow this mind of presence to fill our days. It is much too easy to slide back into old habits once we arise from the cushion. We need to remember to mix the peace of the absorption experienced on the cushion, whatever degree of stillness we experienced that day, with our intention for the hours ahead of us before we return to the cushion again.

To abide in presence demands our honed intention, our commitment, our longing, and a deep and open, accepting curiosity. There is a price for entering the present, for living in it. It entails a letting go of defenses and imaginings, a laying down of self. Selfing occurs at some distance from the present, from here and now.

We can begin to practice presence moment by moment. Chewing, swallowing, showering, walking, sitting, lying down, loading the dryer, getting dialysis or chemo, yawning, crying, bill paying, driving, injecting insulin, writing, reading, talking—especially talking—weeding, vacuuming, breathing.

Breathing is key. It is always available, always centered in the present, always occurring. When we rest within the breath, we find ourselves in awareness with no story. We enter experiential rather than narrative attention. We can ask ourselves, if we wish: am I making this very breath that I am breathing, right now, known? Am I even aware of it arising and abiding and dissolving? Am I taking it for granted? Am I frittering away this moment as I have so many tens of thousands of moments before?

Can I land in this moment? Or will I continue to expend my energy darting around in my own mental images? Can I rest easily in this moment only? Can I rest easily at all? Can I show up now? If not, it is wise to look at what's holding us back, to look at our own resistance to being present.

WE SPEND OUR years in concepts, in a small conceptual life. Our thoughts have become so mesmerizing, our fantasies so fascinating. It's as if we don't want to miss a single act of the inner cinema—we can't wait to get back to it. Until some real time of practice, we prefer its familiar, soap opera banality over the wonder of each new moment.

We have given our thoughts tremendous and compelling power. It takes some effort, often, not to follow their lead. We have become passive to our own habits. The difference between passive and active attention is enormous. Passive attention, unmindful attention, keeps our focus lost in frivolities and inessentials, lost in fictions, lost in far less than our potential. It keeps us asleep. Active attention, focused and simultaneously at ease, is the wisest use of this particular mental faculty of ours. It keeps us awake.

We're all familiar with arriving at a destination with no idea how we got through the stop lights between the point where we arrived and the point where we went blank. We can ask ourselves how many times in all of these decades have we been missing in action, have we not shown up, either for ourselves or for others? What opportunities and experiences have we denied ourselves, lost in our own imaginings? What richnesses have gone unseen and unnoticed?

Are we here now?

We spend our life searching for marvels, minds swirling with memories and possibilities, and miss the ones right here in each and every moment, in life's endless disclosures. Present, we look. Present, we see. Present, we receive and give and be.

The earth's molecules rise up every time our feet make contact with it. Do we notice it? The oxygen that we're breathing in has been shared by seven billion others and offered to us in this breath by the grass and trees and plants around us. How many marvels are we missing?

This life is already a marvel. We are already a marvel. That it all *is* is a marvel. Our trained attention will allow us to recognize this and, then, to embody it, to live it with deepened joy and gratitude, echoing and resounding with the words of the Psalm: "I thank you for the wonder of my being."

Mindful presence not only allows us to stand open before the suffering we may face, adding nothing to it, no story, no self-pity, no reactivity and only the healing mind of compassion; it allows us, also, to deepen and increase our experience of joy.

We can organize our lives around our intention and, within the trajectory of that intention, practice simply showing up. Again, we learn how to be present by practicing being present. Staying with our breath, holding our attention on the breath within the light of our intention, is such a simple and powerful way to actually occupy here and actually occupy now. It keeps us in remembrance, centered in the divine flow, as visionary Christian contemplative Richard Rohr calls it.

Just as each dying person can, in his or her unwavering focus on the breath, we can change our experience of being in a single breath, a single heartbeat. With each mindful breath, each inhalation and exhalation, we can synchronize our micro-rhythm with the larger macro-rhythm, opening into the vastness of being, no longer fractured in our attention, no longer disconnected from all others and from the sacred.

Focusing on the momentary rise and fall of each breath pulls back the veils of distractions and spotlights what is actually happening right now. This is the experience of existing, the simple joy of being. This is a precious human life, so fragile and fleeting. No longer obscured—naked, centered recognition, awake to life's unfolding.

Although it is a vast and luminous everpresence, both our mind's construction of time and the shadow of self obscure Now to only a hidden sliver of light. There's a still point between the "past" and the "future" that we usually ignore. Resting there consciously and consistently, we begin to know the frequency, the vibration of the present. The present is the portal. It's an elusive entrance for passive attention, but the light of it grows brighter, and it widens and opens the more we develop actively mindful attention. It brings us to the vast majesty of our own being.

We hone our mental pliancy and our mindfulness on the cushion in our formal daily practice. We need an off-the-cushion practice, a "remembrance" practice, as well. Otherwise, we're only engaging in transformative practice for the half hour or hour each day of sitting, wasting the rest of our passing minutes and hours. We make a false distinction between holy and mundane.

It's a bit chastening to see how often we can think, after rising from a meditation or sitting or teaching, "Now . . . back to the *real* world." It's important to rise slowly. It's important, if we have so chosen, to remember that the intention to awaken encompasses every moment. No moment can be excluded.

There is, initially in a practice and for quite a long time afterward, a dynamic of compartmentalizing our spiritual life. We rope off many corners and many rooms in that vast, interior castle.

We want to resist that decades-old impulse to fall back into the dream of self, the sleep of form only. It's very helpful to look at the areas of our lives that we wish to cordon off or that we don't choose to view with the eye of spirit. What's off limits? Is it work? Relationships? Family? What we do for relaxation? Is it vanity? Is it attachment? Or grudges? Or fears? Shame or other unhealed aspects of our psyche? It's good to know what we hold as not available for inquiry. There lies our ignorance.

Eventually, as we continue to engage these last years for spiritual practice, we come to see that every moment, every interaction, every circumstance arises from the ground of being. Every moment is one of the places where our feet make contact with the noble path. All of it—the smiles, the wind, the lovemaking, the hearing aid, the knee replacement, the pink slip, the warmth of the sun, the cancer, the scent of lilacs, the funeral, the slip in the snow. It's all part of the path.

This is a wise and skillful view. We want to maintain our best approximation of a wise and skillful view until it arises, through practice, thoroughly, spontaneously, and continuously as an aspect of our being.

APPLYING WHAT WE LEARN in practice, through practice, is to make intelligent use of whatever insight and mindfulness we develop in our daily sitting. When we extrapolate the implications of those insights, gleaned from prayer or meditation or any awakening practice in our daily lives, we create the space for deeper insight, increased mindfulness, and less sleepwalking. Staying mindful of the breath or a chosen word helps to keep us from forgetting what we have been blessed to realize. It keeps us in remembrance.

Unused insights, unused gifts of spirit and spiritual practice, dissipate. They slip out of our grasp. They're often elusive, subtle flashes to begin with. Applying them clarifies them and allows us to embody our realizations. Applying them, we strengthen the imprints of the original insight, keeping it fresh and alive, a living experience rather than a memory. Applying them, we create new neural pathways, new habits. We clear the space for more gifts of spiritual practice when we embody the last gifts and let them flow out through us, sharing them with a generous heart.

We begin to weave together the separation we've mentally created between the spiritual and the worldly. It opens up more rooms in our interior castle. It carries the Sabbath through the week. We find our life becoming a bit more seamless, a bit less fractured, as we begin to abide in wholeness.

Going through an entire day with mindfulness is different from a formal sitting only in terms of the time it occupies. But the process is the same: when our attention wanders, we simply bring it back to mindfulness of the present moment. We drop the deeply embroidered assumptions and the congested energy of selfing—all that will not fit into the open space of the moment—and align in here and now, with this breath.

It's harder to remember and stay mindful as we go about our daily routine's events, certainly. Our days are littered with the triggers of memory and oft-told stories, filled with all the old cues. There's the traffic jams and the leaves that need to be raked and the time spent maintaining all of those possessions we worked so hard to own. There are the relatives and the worries and the annoyances and the bills to pay. There are the illnesses and the fears of illness. There are the intimate arguments, the sinking feelings of overwhelm or loneliness, and the still unfulfilled wishes and unhealed resentments.

We've created the familiar circumstances and scenarios with our patterns, with our unmindfulness. We can fall back into that unmindfulness easily, back into the forgetfulness of our unconscious habit patterns. Unmindfulness has become our default position. We need to change that if we wish to ripen.

As we practice, we will be creating daily landscapes replete with reminders to awaken. If we continue to practice as we age and use this time to become increasingly illuminated, so will our landscapes become increasingly illuminated for us. Each thought, each action, each word, each face viewed and sensation felt will become a reminder that formlessness is functioning through this form. We will begin to live at the zero point of their intersection, at the still point of that mystery. We will, with continued practice, become much more mindful of the nature of each moment our mind creates, much more likely to place our attention beneficially, like a hummingbird who quickly discerns which flowers have nectar.

THE POWER OF meditation is the power of attention used wisely, with coherence and purpose. With training, with attention shepherded by intention, we gather scattered aspects of attention back into awareness. We develop the capacity to ingather and to go deeper, into more inclusive and enveloping dimensions of being.

The relatively simply act, profound in its consequences, of taking the random and disordered waves of ordinary scattered attention and focusing that energy with great unity of purpose creates an entirely new order, a new paradigm, a new being.

In Surat Shabd yoga, the yoga of light and sound, attention is seen as the soul. To train our attention with wisdom is to bring self into soul and then into spirit. To train our attention with wisdom is to allow spirit to shine through self. Ingathered attention, with wise intention and committed practice, can return us to our source. We can think of our attention, tamed and aligned with intention, as the prodigal and always beloved son, returning home.

It is wise to watch our thoughts, simply noting, "thinking, thinking." Thought looks to the past to give itself substance. Thought looks to the future to imagine its own consequence. A mindfulness practice clears the aisles of our stories, clears the space of our imaginings.

With the mind more clear, attachment to our own thoughts decreases. We begin to see thoughts as simply words we've attached to certain neural firings, words we've unmindfully invested with belief. With a transformative practice, attachment to those thoughts suspends for increasing periods of time. And, with that suspension, so, too, do those other fictions of time and self and dualism have the possibility of also being suspended. We're always only a thought away from here and now, and from its great majesty.

This controlled use of the mental faculty of attention, practiced moment by moment in nonreactive witnessing, is mindfulness. We can practice it with the breath, allowing ourselves to show up in our own body, to focus on our sensations, and remove attention from the busy-ness of the mind. We can practice it with a chosen word, replacing the nonsense of our incessant inner monologue with a more meaningful and beneficial sound or statement.

With one breath, one moment of remembrance, our awareness can return to stillness. It can become as still as a mountain that witnesses all that arises before it: clouds and travelers and passing seasons, growing woods, dying woods, woods on fire, rain and rushing streams.

It is our choice where we want to hang out. It is our choice as to where we want to place our attention: in selfing or beyond self. That choice is the only difference between awakened beings and suffering ones.

We can stay lost in the ephemera of distractions and fictions, never showing up, or we can begin to develop and employ the mental pliancy that will allow our awareness to be present and freed. Mental pliancy, the capacity of tamed attention, allows us to release our attachment to the entanglements of our own imaginings, releasing that energy to abide in pure awareness.

Even a month's practice of mindful presence reveals that we all have both the capacity and the agency to choose where to place our attention. It does, however, take a bit of time and cultivation to have the intention to place our attention deliberately, to exercise the mental factor of intention, in every moment.

It is wise to frequently, many times throughout each day, ask ourselves: Is this thought fortifying the delusion of self, or is it freeing attention from self? Does this thought diminish wakefulness or release greater awakening?

Within the multidimensionality of awareness, once we become a bit familiar with awareness beyond self, we can increasingly choose at what level of depth and subtlety we wish to live. We can train our attention to stay centered in peaceful, present equanimity, nonreferential ease, if that is what we choose to cultivate. We can learn to control attention's capacity to zoom and to focus, rather than allowing our unconscious habit patterns to control our perspective for us.

We may encounter fears; indeed, we probably will. Ego's lifelong strategy to avoid presence has kept many of those fears largely unconscious. We may fear that we cannot regain the capacity to be present, that we're too far gone. We may fear that we alone, out of seven billion others, lack the capacity to awaken. This is selfing's thought.

Although we may gracelessly falter over and over again, tumbling back into the dream of self, we must not lose heart. The faltering diminishes in both frequency and intensity over time. Faltering bars no one's entry into awareness beyond self. A friend once shared that she had a very large, very complicated book outlining a diet that needed to be followed down to the last detail. Chapter after chapter explained the intricate ins and outs of it. The last chapter was entitled, "What To Do When You Fall Off the Diet." It had one sentence: "Start over."

We're works in progress. That's worthy of respect. There is great dignity and nobility in the work in progress. And remembrance is only a breath away. We are blessed with an ever-continuing welcome into the timeless awareness of presence. It's an open house, a come-as-you-are party.

> Come, and come again.
> Even if you have broken your troth
> A thousand times . . .
> Come, and come again.
>
> —SUFI PRAYER

WE MAY FEAR that we will remove ourselves from life and connection if we live in present-centered awareness. This is self's ignorance.

To abide in the equanimity of mindfulness does not at all mean that we will remain impassive as we face the challenges of aging and sickness and death and loss. It does not mean that we stoically, unfeelingly, accompany a loved one in his or her dying, for example. Some fear that, without attachment, we will end up in a state of nonfeeling disconnection. This is not at all true. Mindful, we can be utterly present, heart open in deep compassion for our own suffering and the suffering of the other before us—for all suffering. Our capacity to be with suffering increases. We can become whole and present, love pouring out of us.

Each of us has this potential. We are nearing the end of our time to realize it, to directly experience it, to live it.

Some practitioners feel that they've "failed" in their practice if they experience the deep anguish of the loss of a loved one or of their own terminal diagnosis. They then add the pain of that judgment of failure to the pain they already experience. They add salt to their own wounds.

Presence is eminently responsive, attuned, nonjudgmental. Aware presence is vast and unshakeable. It can hold and accept every arising without exception, all of the "blips" of our neural firings. Pain, judgment, ignorance, all arise and dissolve within its equanimity, leaving it as undisturbed as clouds leave sky. It is always open, always welcoming, undismayed by our faltering.

Presence carries an opened heart, not a numbed one. And an opened, present heart can stay open to all experience, including all of the sorrowful aspects of life-in-form. Courageous as well as compassionate, an opened heart radically embraces all of it. An opened heart has such space carved out that it can hold all experience, including our own fears and sorrows and those of others. An opened, present heart can hold such emotions in stillness.

For those of us who are works in progress, even an opening heart arisen from some mental pliancy, has a greater capacity to be present, has more stability to face our challenges. We can, increasingly, sit with anguish, if need be. We can, increasingly, be present with suffering, if need be, with a greater capacity to remain open and compassionate. Our practice can lead us to more ease with undefended vulnerability.

We can practice presence, using our trained mental pliancy. We tie our intention to the stake of the light or the sound or the word or the breath, the focus that keeps us in the moment with no distracting overlays of past or future, no preconceptions, no expectations. Mindfulness keeps us returning to our chosen object. Alertness scans for distractions or diminutions of our clarity and alignment in presence. It alerts us to the tug of self's familiar urges.

Shifting our focus from the frivolity of imaginings and other inessentials, we focus in simplicity. Focused in simplicity, we relax. Relaxing, we let go. Letting go, we reduce reactivity. Reducing reactivity, we become calm. Calmer, we focus more deeply. Focusing more deeply, we experience joy. Experiencing joy, we become single-pointed. Becoming single-pointed, we see. Seeing, we grow in wisdom and compassion and break the chains that bind us. Breaking the chains that bind us, we release awareness into beyond-self. Releasing awareness into beyond-self, we embody a boundless and generous heart.

WE HAVE ALL grown up with the awareness that we are only using and experiencing the tiniest percentage of our capacities. We have heard that we only use ten percent of our mind. Perhaps as school children, we pictured our brain with only one tenth of the circuits going off and actually functioning, wondering how to activate the other ninety percent of the dormant circuits, as if they were unused real estate. We took it as a quantitative notion, not a qualitative one.

The truth is we've only brushed the surface of our potentials.

With a disciplined spiritual path, we begin to harmonize the circuitry, to fine-tune it with noble minds. We rewire the brain with newly forged pathways that can begin to let the self-referential loop weaken in atrophy, that can begin to move beyond conceptuality. With a disciplined spiritual path, we begin to create awareness as beautiful symphony, a confluence of all of the noble minds and noble uses of our precious endowment as human beings. We can begin to know the mind of formless clear light, the ultimate confluence, living always here, always now, always in a prayer of communion, always undefended, always present.

Our focused concentration of attention on our chosen anchor is a powerful catalyst of transformation and awakening, just as the focused, present-centered attention on the breath is for those who are dying. This sustained focus on the breath may engender, for many dying people, the first time that they actually, fully, showed up in their lives. There's sadness and great poignancy in the thought of so many missed opportunities in the lives of those whose fleeting experience of the awakened state is only at the time of death.

To show up, though, to finally be present, even if belatedly at the eleventh hour, allows those at the end of life to enter the grace in dying. There are many who have not had much of an opportunity to mindfully occupy the present moment until the very, very end of life with anything other than fear or raw instincts for survival. Millions exist in conflict-torn or famine-plagued or disease-ridden conditions on our planet. There are many who came to the end of life with neither the opportunity palliative care can provide nor the inclination nor the instruction about how to show up, how to occupy this life in the presence of the sacred. All that this human life offers remained, for one reason or another, unavailable to them, inaccessible to them, until the transformations of the dying process at the very end of their lives.

We can learn from this. There are powerful implications in the poignant understanding that many people do not have the opportunities in their lives to heal and grow and practice and flourish, until life's very last moment. It is profoundly good fortune to be able to pursue a spiritual path while still in the midst of life.

We can deepen our determination to awaken beyond self during this time of our aging and engage in steadfast practice, if we wish. We can offer the fruits of our awakening in the name of all those who have already died and for all those who have yet to die without the blessings of a practice.

> May all beings everywhere
> with whom we are inseparably connected
> and who want and need the same as we do,
> may all be liberated, healed, fulfilled, and free.
>
> —Lama Surya Das

May we, as a generation that was offered the profound gift of spiritual teachings from every tradition, as well as the freedom and opportunity to practice those teachings, fully show up in our lives. May we fully show up far before the last moments allotted to us. May we—as Ram Dass, one of our own most beloved elders, invited us—be here now and share the quiet refuge of presence with a suffering world.

COMMITMENT

LIBERATION FROM DECEPTION

When intention transforms into commitment and comes together with a trained attention that is able to actually be present, to actually show up in each moment, there arises an especially powerful confluence of the circumstances that facilitate awakening.

Our commitment to our practice, to engaging in awakening into awareness beyond self, beyond form alone, is a key element for those who wish to use these last years as a retreat. This is the commitment Joseph Goldstein, a revered American Dharma teacher, refers to as "taking the one seat": the committed, deliberate, sustained application of our attention with intention. It is another of the conditions that fosters spiritual ripening.

For the dying, this committed practice of bringing attention to the present moment occurs on the hospital bed. It is choiceless. For those of us who still have breaths and time remaining to us, it's our commitment to practice each day, all day—or at least as much of the day as we remember to be mindfully present. It's our commitment to keep the organizing principle of each of our days as our intention to awaken.

To MAKE AND KEEP this commitment is a liberation from many of our own deceptions. To make and keep this commitment, we must have already come to some recognition of the truth of impermanence. We must have dropped the deceptive belief that our happiness depends upon circumstances. We must have already come to some clear recognition that it is the ignorance of selfing alone that is the cause of our suffering and the obstruction to the freedom of our own vast and utterly fulfilled essential nature.

To make this commitment, we must have already asked ourselves, as many already have, what is the most meaningful use of this time in my life? And we need to have answered our own question with some honesty and with some wisdom.

One friend's answer was that he wanted to make sure he learned the lessons offered to him in this lifetime, because he sure didn't want to have to repeat them. Another friend asked such questions and realized that nothing except using these last years to awaken held any attraction or made any sense for her. Yet another, deeply committed to her practice and her own awakening, calls it "the only thing that's left—nothing else even comes close to mattering." One friend shared, "I'm seventy-seven. And since I've moved this intention to the center of my life, I've never felt younger or more alive."

Keeping the commitment to awaken enables a liberation from wavering in our intention as well as a liberation from laziness and discouragement, from our half-heartedness and self-deceit. It signals that, although we may continue to struggle with them, we have let go of enough feelings of unworthiness to recognize that every living being, including ourselves, has the capacity to awaken.

Taking the one seat in the midst of life involves making our own chosen commitment choiceless. Committing to using our last years as a time of awakening forces us to stop running mindlessly through our allotted breaths and actually show up in our lives. At our age, it's hardly too soon to take this precious opportunity seriously—though this is not to say that we must take it heavily. There is joy in true commitment. There is ease and relaxation and a growing simplicity and lightness.

Our commitment indicates that we are willing to let go of our frivolity and our attachment to inessentials. It doesn't mean that we've let go of it already; it means we're committed to letting go.

Our commitment expresses our willingness to become authentic, to have our word mean something, to have our attention show up with our body. Having a strong commitment to awaken into awareness beyond self does not mean that we won't fall back into the self's unconscious habit patterns—or sometimes even feel that they're enjoyable. The commitment to awaken is simply to return to the commitment to awaken, over and over.

Looking at where we are attached, where we place our attention, what holds us back from ever-present awareness, is more than worth the effort it takes. Gradually, we can wean ourselves from our childish squandering of potential and bring more and more of the moments of our lives under the umbrella of our intention.

Making a commitment to awaken is an act that reflects growing spiritual maturity. It arises from the realization that the only work to be done is the work of transforming our own mind. It arises from the realization that we must own our own practice. There is no cheating with this homework. No one else can do it for us.

When we understand that we must actually practice, that we must actually become practitioners, we act on that understanding. It is like finally placing a rudder in a boat that has been drifting and tossing in the waves for a long time.

Taking the one seat is our commitment to mindfulness and awakening. We observe our habitual patterns mindfully, managing them with the higher energy level of mindfulness. We observe them nonjudgmentally, without reactivity, with only compassion for the suffering that they have caused us and have caused others.

Adopting a spiritual path hardly ends uncomfortable feeling

states. Initially, it may well highlight them. It exposes to our own view the destructive states of mind that have afflicted us for decades.

This is where keeping the one seat matters. The discipline part of a spiritual discipline involves returning ourselves again and again, time after time, to the practice, especially when we've become lost in our own fictions and imaginings, contracted and tense. With this discipline, we can reshape our habit patterns, adding creativity to karma. In doing so, we create the causes for future moments to generally unfold with less suffering, simply because there is less self-cherishing and self-grasping as we continue in our practice.

We commit to being mindful, alert, conscientious, wakeful.

> In the garden of gentle sanity,
> May you be bombarded by coconuts of wakefulness.
>
> —Chogyam Trungpa

The wish to awaken to awareness beyond self is the light that guides our actions, if we so choose. We commit to our own longing, commit to the practices that will give rise to the fulfillment of our longing. We somehow find a way to love the coconuts.

In northern climes in times gone by, many of the farmers and homesteaders would hang a rope from the house to the barn. In snowstorms, they could use the rope to go back and forth between the two places, doing what needed to be done. They always had the rope to guide them to one place or the other in a blizzard's white out. Our commitment to taking the one seat is our rope. It will guide us back home.

Our consistent and sustained application of attention leads to stability of practice. It enables a growing capacity to just be, to enter awareness bare of self-reference, and allow attention to finally abide in the deeply absorbed, subtle, and formless dimensions of the sacred.

This process demands our patience, our confidence, our humility, and our tested faith. Brother Lawrence, a seventeenth-century French monk, committed his life to the practice of being in the presence of God. His attentional training involved conversing with God continuously and referring all he did to God. To Brother Lawrence, being in God's presence was like holding the rope in a snow storm. He confirmed that, in the beginning, applying his mind to God took some diligence. In time and "after a little care," he found that the love that he felt from God, as he abided in God's presence with love, inwardly excited him to continuous practice "without any difficulty."

Over time, effort begins to become joyful, in the same way that the work of planning for a vacation can be joyful or cooking for our lover or our child can be a joy-filled task. Wise effort becomes ease, a wonder, a delight. At some point, we don't want our mind to abide anywhere other than in ever-present awareness. This is when all of our life becomes a retreat. Every moment is seen as meditation.

THERE ARE NOT many caves or isolated huts in the United States. There are not that many convents and monasteries left standing. Most of us will do the retreats of our old age in our own homes—or in a hospital or in a nursing home. One elderly nun spent a great deal of her last years in the front room of a single-wide trailer. If someone asked her how she was, she always replied with the same answer: "Jesus and I are so much in love." Another friend, mid-seventies, is doing her retreat as she wanders around the world with a single backpack, connecting with others wherever she goes, stopping to meditate wherever the shelter is offered, even if that shelter be the night sky.

The setting for our retreat doesn't matter. A retreat is really a state of mind in which every moment is held as a moment of awakening, because we have chosen it to be so. This choice and this commitment allow us to let go of every inessential and every deceptive fiction, keeping our attention abiding more and more in ever-present awareness, open to everything just as it is, without the ego's itch to embroider.

This is a gift we can give ourselves and our loved ones and the world with the wise use of our older years.

We practice presence in as many moments as we can remember to do so. This is our remembrance practice throughout each day. We grow in our capacity to abide here, to be now, to allow mindfulness. Our curiosity and our capacity for naked inquiry grow. We begin to be able to investigate the self to which we have for so long identified and clung, with more honesty and detachment and wonder.

What is it that I call "me"? What is its nature? We can experience the sense of self, the burden of self, thinning under such inquiry, such analytic questioning. When we actually look, we begin to actually see. What we see is the absence of what we thought was there.

WE CAN TAKE heart in the fact that so many tens of thousands have traveled the path before us, leaving us with their affirming knowledge that there are proven paths and that there is a known process of awakening.

In whatever tradition resonates with us, we fabricate a view of the path we wish to follow. We then apply and engage in practice according to the instructions of that view. Buddhism offers a view that helps to give us a sense of where we are on the path of awakening, no matter which tradition's path we're on. It is a view of progressive stages that can serve to encourage us. It can also highlight where we need to place our attention next if we are to realize our longing for spiritual maturity.

Buddhism speaks of five bodhisattva paths. These are the paths of accumulation, preparation, seeing, meditation, and no more learning. To define a Buddhist term in such a way that its meaning can become clear in any tradition, we can say that a bodhisattva is one from any tradition who is motivated by love and compassion and wisdom, one who is committed to abandoning self-reference and its deceptions and imaginings.

The only requirements for the designation "bodhisattva," as we are using it here, are those of motivation and commitment. We do not need to have perfected our love and wisdom and compassion. We do not need to have already abandoned self-reference. We do not need to have a mind free from stories and habit patterns.

We start with our experience of whatever is arising for us at the moment and our reaction to that arising. We start nowhere else but here, nowhere else but now. The challenges, the struggles, the reactions we encounter on our way are the steppingstones of the path. There would be no path without them.

To enter these paths, which is to say to embark upon a life of spiritual deepening or awakening, we do need to have already established in our minds and hearts certain understandings that have become real for us. Some groundwork needs to have been done or we wouldn't even be considering entering such a fortunate path, such a precious path leading us to the infinite.

Often, this groundwork arises out of pain at the level of the heart. Our groundwork can arise from an illness, an unexpected loss (what losses do we every truly and totally expect?), a disenchantment with much that had previously held our attention, or a growing lack of interest in the inessential, the superficial. Often it arises out of a deep intuitive understanding that life has greater freedom and purpose and meaning than we have experienced thus far in all of these decades. That intuitive understanding nurtures a deep longing for that greater purpose, that greater meaning and freedom.

Part of the groundwork necessary to enter a spiritual path in earnest, rather than just in flirtation, involves a measure of pondered life experience. As people in our sixties, seventies, and eighties, we certainly meet the requirement for a measure of life experience. If we have not done so before, we will want to also meet the requirement of having pondered it, having extracted some wisdom from it. The necessary groundwork also involves some small relinquishment of our tight attachment to self, left over from all of the years of clinging to it. Many of us are just plain tired of living in such tense contraction.

To step onto the path of a bodhisattva, one who is committed to cultivating the most noble and sane of qualities, we need to have already understood the painful nature of stress and unease and confusion as they exist in our own lives. We need to have already felt a strong desire to lessen our susceptibility to their seduction, ultimately to be free of them. This is renunciation.

We need to have contemplated the nature of human existence a bit, to have zoomed back in our view to a larger and expanded picture that allows us to understand the painful nature of stress and unease and confusion as they exist in the minds of all other beings. We need to feel a strong and wholehearted longing that all other beings, too, be free of those unsatisfiable and destructive afflictions and the hells they create. This is compassion.

These are two powerful minds, renunciation and compassion. The mind of renunciation is the wish to be free from the painful attachment to the illusions and deceptions of self, recognizing that attachment as the origin of suffering. The mind of compassion recognizes our commonality with all others. The mind of compassion begins to genuinely wish all others to also be free of suffering, just as we wish to be.

If we choose to move along a path of awakening, we make an inner commitment. This commitment, one that often arises spontaneously in moments of deep contemplation, is to contribute the fruits of our own spiritual practice to the goal of lessening the suffering of the world. There begins to arise spontaneously the wish to share the joy of a boundless heart with all others, to begrudge it to no one. With the tenderly growing new minds of renunciation and compassion, we begin to become more of a blessing to ourselves and others, more of a being through whom light begins to shine.

These understandings, deeply felt, are the understandings that establish the intention for our practice. They are the very foundations of our practice. The mind of renunciation and the mind of compassion are strengthened when they are mixed with the mind of the love of God, for example, or when they are mixed with the deep intuition that awakening is, in fact, available to us, that we all have the seed of buddhanature. Otherwise, without intimations of and invitations from beyond-self, we would deeply see and feel suffering but be stuck with it forever.

When those two minds of renunciation and compassion begin to arise spontaneously, in an unlabored way, we are ready to consciously enter the noble paths of a bodhisattva.

WE ENTER the path because we aspire and intend to awaken.

We can drop any image we may have of what a bodhisattva looks like and experiences and thinks and feels. The bodhisattva we are looks like and experiences and thinks and feels like us. One can rest easy in the knowledge that it is a humbling, fumbling, bumbling process for all. However the path is for each of us who is awakening, that is how awakening is for us. Having taken refuge in our own deepest wisdom and goodness, we can trust that we have begun to rest in the divine flow and that it always will, as it always has, carry us within it.

On the paths of a bodhisattva, the speed of awakening revs up, having added the fuel of causes and conditions, having announced that we're ready, or at least getting ready, for the formless ground of being to reveal itself. Consciously recognizing that awakening has always been our trajectory, we accelerate arising from the dream of self. We begin to see that the unfolding of awareness can never be anywhere other than on that trajectory. No matter how many side trips or detours, the path of return to the sacred, to our essential nature, is the arc of all of our journeys. Nisargadatta, the great nondual sage, reminds us that liberation is a natural process, an inevitable process, and a process within our power "to bring it into the Now."

Stepping consciously onto the path, we change the direction of our lives. We begin the task of reshaping our karmic habits to turn toward beyond-self. We begin to apply our entire being to the holy work and, as we do so, we move toward the fulfillment of our longing to make the last years of our lives ones of deep and beautiful meaning and purpose.

The spontaneous arising of renunciation and compassion, however limited, however quickly sinking like stones beneath the ocean of old habit patterns, allows us to begin to have something real upholding us. We begin to approach genuine ground. These two minds of renunciation and compassion are filled with truth and goodness and beauty. They have a reality. They approach a groundedness, a capacity to uphold our spiritual progress. None of all of our previous stories and fictions and imaginings, although they gave the illusion of ground, could ever measure up to the task. They are, and always have been, deceptive.

These spontaneously arising minds of renunciation and compassion grow and mature as we proceed, eventually to become not only spontaneous but also thorough and continuous. They are powerful minds and they feed and amplify each other and amplify the wise effort we apply in our spiritual practice.

THE FIRST PATH we enter on a consciously chosen spiritual journey within any wisdom lineage is called, in Buddhism, *the path of accumulation*. Here we actively, and as wholeheartedly as we are able, accumulate and gather together the causes and conditions for our own awakening. We accumulate learning and studying and practice instructions. The wisdom of others, to which we attend and upon which we contemplate, opens our minds further. We begin to relax some of the tightness of our previously held conceptions and convictions. Clearing out much of what we think we know—not always an easy process because we are so graspingly convinced of the truth of our own imaginings—we create the space for some sprouts of wisdom to take root.

We accumulate merit. Merit can be said to be the cultivation of minds that further our intention, as well as the gradual elimination of the old habituated minds that have kept us trapped and limited for so long. The path of accumulation is a period of development, prior to the discovery or revelation of our own deepest nature. We need development, the creation of space increasingly freed of self-cherishing and self-grasping. Self-reference cannot endure the light of naked holiness discovered.

The path of accumulation is a period of deliberately looking at the haphazard and destructive flood of habit patterns in our own mind, and of beginning to provide some riverbanks and levees where there were none before.

This process occurs on the cushion first. With mindfulness, we sit observing what has been going on in our minds all along. This witnessing demands honesty, the increasing capacity, grown through commitment, to hold nothing back from inquiry and from letting go. We are opening ourselves to chaos.

Sitting with our own thoughts and feelings and memories and desires can be painful. The more mindful is our witnessing, the more shadowy aspects of our psyche will be observed. This demands courage, along with honesty and exquisitely tender compassion. Approaching the truth can be fearful for the self. To open to truth, we first need to let go of our false securities. There are times of feeling vulnerable and scared—even despairing.

We keep sitting. We sit in the knowledge that this is a part of the process of healing from our fractured state and becoming whole. This is part of the process of letting go of all of the snagging points of selfing.

What have we done that we regret having done? What have we not done that we regret not having done? Who have we hurt, in addition to ourselves? Can we allow ourselves to feel remorse and enter, as others have done before, this rite of passage? Can we then let go? Can we leave the baggage of the past behind and show up in the present, chastened and lighter and more free?

As we sit, witnessing the wounds, the experience can be both heart-breaking and humbling. As Ajahn Chah, the revered Theravadin Buddhist teacher put it, "if we haven't wept deeply, we haven't begun to meditate." One friend shared that one of her deepest meditations was one where she saw that she had, in ways both large and small, harmed every single loved one in her life. Tears poured down her cheeks for a few hours, she said, in this cleansing and releasing and purifying experience.

This weeping is a rite of passage. It is the purification that compassionate remorse can effect. It can take some time. As much as we may want to awaken, we often find it difficult to let go. The growing wisdom and clarity that finally releases our attention's tight grasp on our past indicates that we have emerged more into the present. Letting go is liberating.

Over time, we develop the capacity to observe the contents of our mind with less reactivity, neither judging nor engaging in whatever fictions arise. But we need to allow ourselves to touch our sorrows and our fears first. To touch them, to embrace them, to heal them, clears the space for the further work that needs to be done. In all likelihood, sorrows and fears will arise again. Each time they do, to sit with them, with eyes weeping and heart softening, we heal on deeper and deeper levels.

At this point in our spiritual path, even sitting for a half an hour can be a challenge as we struggle with the chaos of difficult emotions and with boredom. A focal object of attention, such as the breath or a chosen word or the determination to witness each new arising, is important. It allows us to continually ingather every time we scatter. Our nonvolitional afflictive emotions, as they arise, become the very signal for intention to return attention to the refuge of deliberate mindfulness.

We can think of intentional, ingathered attention as a light through which to see. Martin Laird, who teaches a deep and beautiful method of contemplation within the Christian tradition, speaks of the light through which we see at this stage of awakening as like the light of a torch. We shine it where we have not shone it before, exploring much that has been hidden in the inner caverns.

On this first path of a genuine spiritual journey, we learn to sit with our thoughts and feelings and, stepping back into the observing awareness, explore whether or not we are those thoughts and feelings. With the slightest bit of dis-identification that begins to arise, we can shepherd the energy of the thoughts and feelings, often destructive and always fictitious, rather than having them shepherd us.

For most people, time on the path of accumulation is a time of abandoning first our outwardly harmful actions. We seek first of all to become harmless in the world. We engage in the practice of moral discipline, a sane and joyful practice of not harming.

This practice of harmlessness helps us to gain the confidence and discriminating wisdom to become more harmless in the intimate depths of our own being. We train in wise speech and wise livelihood and wise action—the outward management of remaining habit patterns—while, at the same time, deepening wise intention and wise view. Each of the applications of wisdom functions interdependently, each wisdom amplifying the other.

In accordance with our intention, most of us will work on managing the destructive minds that beset us for a long time. We should be prepared; it's a gradual task. These habit patterns do not disappear overnight, nor do they disappear through magical thinking or wishful thinking or lip-synching mantras or aspirations.

> All the time I pray to Buddha,
> I keep on
> killing mosquitoes.
>
> —Issa

As it was for Issa, a nineteenth-century Zen practitioner, so it is for many of us now. At this point on the path, we may not even be half-baked. We can take heart in the examples of persistence and perseverance of those who have gone before us. We all need to tap into our own conscientiousness, our "immaculate integrity," as Don Juan, the Mexican shaman, called it, and mindfully apply that conscientiousness.

The path of accumulation is a time of preparing the field. In both our sitting and our remembrance practice throughout the day, we begin the task of removing stones and weeds. We work the soil of our mind, with the intention of softening its hardened fabrications and imaginings, dis-identifying with them the while.

Accumulating merit assists in reshaping our karmic patterns so that future moments allow even greater growth in freedom and in all of our most noble qualities. These noble qualities are able to shine through us as our own essential being when attachment to selfing lessens. Our locus of identification shifts.

There comes a point in the path of accumulation when we have gathered "enough" of what we need to know to begin to take ownership and accountability for our own practice and inquiry with deep sincerity. We don't carry the need to memorize every sutra or to read the lives of every saint or to learn one more practice or get one more empowerment. Although there is much wisdom yet to be grown and known, at some point toward the end of the path of accumulation, we have gathered enough of the wisdom of listening and studying and contemplating to go more deeply on the path.

There is a moment, a beautiful transitional moment, when the implications of all of the wisdom we have accumulated through listening and studying become real for us. We take them in thoroughly. We take them to heart.

In that moment of transition, however long it may last, we, in a deeply embodied, directly known recognition, realize that we have deep, thorough, genuine, heartfelt respect for the path and for ourselves for engaging in the path. We are no longer looking for validation or acceptance or praise for being on the path. Commitment deepens. We begin to cease looking outwardly for rescue. Turning inward, resting inwardly, begins to become more natural. We change what is familiar.

Nothing matters as much as going more deeply into our own being and working in the fields of our own mind. We begin to take personal responsibility for intimately applying the teachings and their implications to our own lives, to our own minds. Our wanting, our spiritual desire, deepens. At this beautiful turning point, we enter the second path, the path of preparation.

EARNESTNESS IS KEY. Earnestness, sincerity, our own deep thirst, open the way into the path of preparation.

We deepen our sincerity. We may have thought that we were

sincere before, but this is earnestness at a whole new level. This earnestness hungers for Dharma, for the truth, for our own sake and for the sake of all others. It is committed to rooting out all deception. With this new earnestness of the path of preparation, we begin to practice with more wise effort than ever before and with wise and deepening concentration.

The path of preparation is practicing for real. We train the mind in deeper and deeper absorption so that concentrated energy can be used for seeing clearly into the nature of all things, including the self.

We deepen our capacity to let go of our fictions and their powerful, knee-jerk emotionality. We rest more nonreactively in our ability and willingness to let things, and others, be—just as they are. Patient acceptance and the capacity to be present begin to more firmly take root and send out some felt indications of their rootedness.

We begin to be able to sit in greater ingathering, concentration, and equanimity. We grow in our ability to offer that peace to those around us, and we wish to do so, as generosity grows within our being.

The striving of ego diminishes further and chaos begins to give way to surrender. Both the willingness to let formlessness reveal itself and the faith that it *will* begin to grow. The seeking that obscures finding diminishes. Martin Laird describes the light of our capacity to see at this point in our awakening as like the light of moonlight, where all appears less substantial.

With less of selfing's obstructions confusing us, we transform, as many journeyers have noted, from the victim of what is happening to the observer of what is happening. This is the beginning of an immense transformation, the cessation of taking everything personally.

We take our believing out of the accounts of our fictions and imaginings and rest in increasing stillness. We're no longer willing to engage in deceptions and denial, seeing those ploys very clearly as the obstructions they are. We become increasingly responsible for what we allow to form.

Healing and purification occur as we increasingly align in our more trained attention. We let go more, release more, shedding the unreal and the inessential. We ride the waves of whatever is arising with increasing ease. Our mindfulness becomes more unruffled as our self-reference and all of its attachments and aversions decrease.

Healing and purification occur in our once fractured and besieged psyche. As healing leads us toward wholeness, we begin to discern the self-grasping and self-cherishing at the root of every pattern, the barriers that have always blocked the simple joy of being. We begin to rest, with increasing stability, in the hallowed, living awareness from which all arises.

THIS GROWING CAPACITY to rest in awareness that observes not only the afflictive emotions besetting the self but also the self that feels beset places us right at the edge of the third path, the path of seeing.

We practice maintaining the silence and absorption of deeply concentrative states, beyond words and beyond self. At first we are only able to maintain the absorption for a few moments, a few breaths. With practice in placing and replacing—continuously placing—the attention, we eventually cultivate the ability to direct and keep our attention on our chosen object of focus indefinitely. This is called *tranquil abiding* or *calm abiding*, the wordless inner prayer of the heart.

Although we can work diligently to attain this meditative or contemplative absorption and equipoise, we want to remember that its attainment depends upon diligence's balance with ease. We want to remember to deliberately and thoroughly set up that ease and that relaxation of body and emotions and mind from the very beginning of sitting down for our daily practice. Doing so, we have created the causes and gathered the conditions for insight.

From this concentrated mind, as concentrated as a laser, we can see. Looking for the self, deeply searching, we cannot find it. This is a moment of deep experiential knowing, a wordless shock of insight. This insight is seeing. It is such a profound moment on anyone's spiritual path that, from that moment on, ordinary conceptions, which take appearances to exist in the way that they seem to a fabricating mind, are forever vanquished. That paradigm simply vanishes, much as a mirage vanishes upon close investigation.

This is a sublime attainment. In it, we know ourselves to be none other than the silence and the empty fullness of present-centered awareness. We are free of grasping to a self, free of the limitations of attachment to a self. We see through the self. We see it as the fiction it is. We awaken from the long, deluded dream. We see, also, the "self" of all that we've imputed as fiction, as mere imputation.

This moment of direct realization is the moment of entry into the third path, the path of seeing, a seeing from beyond self. It is the entrance into transcendence, the radiant space where noble qualities come to fruition.

In some ways, it could be said that that this single moment of deeply piercing insight, of direct knowing, is the whole of the path of seeing. Thoughts, feelings, and the self felt to experience them are all seen to be empty of inherent existence, diaphanous appearings arising from the ground of being, ephemeral forms coarising with the formless. Laird refers to the light with which we see here as sunlight, illuminating everything, revealing the "sunlit absence" of illusions.

Thoughts and feelings continue to arise since habitual patterns are deeply ingrained. We begin, though, to recognize that they are of one taste with the vast and luminous awareness in which they arise. This is the transformation of ignorance into wisdom.

We begin our practice in almost total ignorance. Perhaps for most of us, we begin in complete and utter ignorance, but with hunger, with longing, with an intuition. Unmindful and fairly lost in the confusion of ignorance, we identify with the contents of awareness. Our experience of self is not other than the contents of awareness.

From the relative freedom gained with the mindful ability to dis-identify with the contents of awareness, to simply witness them, we become familiar with awareness itself. At this point, we hold the experience of awareness and the experience of its contents as separate.

And then we come full circle. With our identity released from attachment to self and with attention resting in awareness, we finally come to experience, on the path of seeing, awareness and its contents, the objects of awareness, arising simultaneously. They co-arise in interdependence, the one taste of each moment's arising.

> First there is a mountain,
> then there is no mountain,
> then there is.
>
> —DONOVAN, TRANSLATING D. T. SUZUKI

Jack Kornfield brings this insight home even more pointedly, more practically: "After the ecstasy, the laundry." First there is a dirty sock, then there is no dirty sock, and then it still needs washing.

Awareness and objects of awareness are a single display, form and formlessness dancing to the rhythm of impermanence. With that realized awareness arises a new world and a new being, an awakened being. We will still need to fold the warm clothes from the dryer, engaging in life-in-form but now conscious, now awake.

THERE ARE SUBTLE and beautiful stages of progression into deeper and more inclusive and luminous dimensions of awareness, even beyond the path of seeing. In traditional Buddhist teachings, the fourth path, the path of meditation, follows the path of seeing. In this path, whatever subtle boundaries remain between life and death are healed and we are freed from even the imprints of attachment. The boundaries between self and other, however subtly lingering, like the scent of a box that once held incense, are also healed and we are freed from duality.

The path of meditation is like the rinse cycle on a washing machine, making sure that even the lightest traces of impurity are cleansed. The moment of their complete removal is called, in Tibetan Buddhist tradition, "the mind of vajra-like concentration." This moment is the absolute and final and irreversible cessation of any mind other than the most noble.

THE VAST RADIANCE of formless awareness shines forth in all its immaculate glory, and we enter the fifth path, the path of no more learning. Awake. Being is illuminated. Being is experienced at the zero point, the balanced intersection between form and formlessness. The light of reality seen and known here is described in Tibetan Buddhist tradition as "clear light." In American Buddhist teacher Robert Thurman's lovely phrase, "we swim in the infinite," the ground of being.

A view of the five paths gives us a sense of the way before us. It can inspire us, it can give us direction, it can give us hope. Even the fact that the path is known because it has been followed into its fulfillment by others can give us encouragement. It can deepen our commitment.

Now we just need to sit and practice.

WE WILL NOTE in ourselves, from the time of our initial commitment and as we continue in earnest and committed practice, an increased capacity to be present, to show up in our meditations and in our lives.

Recognizing that our experience is utterly dependent upon where we place our attention, we begin to shape a life filled with more love, more harmony, more beauty, more generosity. This is not to say that we can escape the predictable sufferings of a human existence, but we can completely transform the way we relate to each moment of this life-in-form, including its last.

We can choose to cultivate the Pure Land of the present moment.

> This very earth
> is the Lotus Land of Purity;
> and this body
> is the body of the Buddha.
>
> —Hakuin

This experience is available to us. Martin Laird likens it to sinking into God's being. David Steindl-Rast calls it "God bathing." This peaceful mind, cultivated in practice, is what we have to offer to ourselves and to each other and to a world that badly needs peace, a world that is the very exposition of what unpeaceful minds create.

Abiding in presence, we cease dissipating the pure energy arising in each moment. We are no longer so unmindful as to allow our conceptions and fabrications to get away with congesting and diminishing the energy of the ground of being. Our habit patterns can find no traction in pure energy, and we are no longer so willing to allow them to take form. We develop the capacity to simply witness them with more equanimity as they make their appearances.

We become increasingly familiar with simply being. Kindness arises naturally out of awareness that has gone through enough training to show up in the present moment. Our own kindness, the kindness of our own essential nature, is unveiled as we let go of some of our self-cherishing and self-absorption. Lovingkindness begins to fill us and allows our cup to runneth over.

In this centered awareness, replete with noble qualities ripening, we are able, finally, to be available in a beneficial way for the awakening of everyone, ourselves and others. Even while we are still works in progress, we have more to give. Even half-baked, our being is expanded. Equanimity and love and compassion and the genuine authenticity, the wholeness, of presence become available to offer.

We position ourselves interpersonally in more appropriate and healthy ways. There is an appropriate point of positioning in the dance we do with each person. Too close, and we're likely to feed attachment or aversion. Too far, and we're likely to feed indifference. It is a delicately nuanced point of mindful placement that allows us and the other to simply be, to simply be present together.

The gift of our attention becomes possible when we have practiced training our attention. This gift of attention is the most underused of human resources. That's sad. It's one of the most precious things we have to offer each other. There are many times that each of us has not been fully present with another, occupied with our own thoughts or our own perceived needs or our own manufactured agendas. There have been many times that we have disregarded another for the sake of our own self-cherishing.

We can ask: Do I still mimic the postures of kindness as defense or plea or bargaining point? What is my resistance to freely offering my heartfelt and complete attention and presence to another? Am I willing to give the gift of my attention? The answer to that last question is important. That willingness is directly related to our own happiness and our own awakening.

As we progress along our path of ripening, our encounters with others can be increasingly filled with meaning and with benefit and with lovingkindness. We're here to learn from each other. The capacity to share both joy and sorrow, laughter and anguish, is an indication of our growing spaciousness. We enter tender communion in a more subtle, greatly healed wholeness, filled with meaning not so much in doing but in being.

Ram Dass has a lovely insight: "We're all just walking each other home." We're here to share with each other, to comfort and be comforted, to be present with each other as we arise from the sleep of ignorance. There's an old joke about God saying, "that's why I made more than one of you."

The gift of attention is compassionate presence. The Tibetan word for "presence" is *wangthang*. It translates as "field of power." Because of the intensity of that field of power, we can sense presence, our own or another's or the two conjoined, and find great stability within it.

To be present, to consciously be a presence, to consciously offer our presence as a field of power holding our most positive and noble qualities, demands that we have done a great deal of emptying-out work, of releasing. It demands that we are well on our way to clearing the field of delusions, afflictive emotions, and attachment to self. Presence, as the field of power, is a powerful absence of self-reference.

The gift of attention becomes more freely available to pass around when we have trained in mindful attending and, with committed intention, left the inessential and the unreal behind. The less selfing, the greater the gift is our presence. Everyone benefits.

Unless we are the first to die in our close circle of family and friends, it is certain that we will sit with dying loved ones. May we be able, at that time, to give them the gift of attention, opened and ripened into sweetness by our wise intention and wise effort.

May we have so cultivated our own spiritual ripening that we are able to be present with another's suffering—or joy or difficult decision, for that matter—without shutting down. May we be able to offer our own compassionate presence without controlling, or inflating our ego, without denial, without confusion.

May we develop the capacity to continue to be present with another where we might ordinarily have contracted back into our own pain and fear or need for answers. May we have so cultivated our own spiritual ripening that we can allow ourselves to receive the gifts of another's compassionate presence.

May we deepen our intention to ripen in whatever time remains to us.

MINDFUL OF EACH BREATH, in as much as we remember, our remembrance will grow. Mindful of each breath, we increase our capacity to show up in our lives, to be present for what is essential. We stay present in now, grounded in here, living in the fullness of form and formlessness, firmly planted in the realization from Psalm 139: "Where could I go from your Spirit?"

We will come to deeply know that there is nowhere to go except more deeply into tender communion with all that is, where lives and deaths are inhaled and exhaled in breaths without number.

This is wholeheartedness of presence, arisen from commitment, the gift of attention that we give to ourselves and to the world. In it, we are free from the dream of self and its weighty and unsettling distractions and its soporific deceptions. We live in clarity as the lenses of our old false paradigms no longer distort each freshly arising moment. We live in interbeing, wishing each other awakening.

> In wholeheartedness of presence,
> the Buddha is realized,
> the Dharma is lived
> and the Sangha is shared.
> —DAININ KATAGIRI

LIFE REVIEW AND RESOLUTION

LIBERATION FROM OUR STORY; RELEASE INTO FREEDOM

> What do you have to do?
>
> Pack your bags,
> Go to the station without them,
> Catch the train,
> And leave your self behind.
>
> —Wei Wu Wei

Life review is a vivid inner experience. In this work, which seems to arise naturally in the minds of those who are in the endstages of a terminal illness, thousands of bubbles of memories are sorted through as part of the long goodbye. Often for the first time, the memories are opened up to and understood and accepted.

Sharing this process can often have great benefit for both the dying person and his or her loved ones. Sometimes such life review can bring up turmoil and unresolved familial conflict, but most often, shared with others, it leads to a healing. It allows a deepened understanding of the bond that has been created in the connection of love. It allows grateful, humbling, and forgiving recognition of all of the thousands of moments of love that, together, have forged that bond.

Out of seven billion people on earth, these few are my family; these few are my intimate friends and loved ones. These are the ones with whom I've most closely shared this precious and fleeting existence.

As life review is undertaken at the end of life—and this does not necessarily have to be done formally—the gratitude for our inner karmic circle can be immense. Love and gratitude and forgiveness are often so present—and render us so vulnerable—that, at times, it is almost more than one can bear. The experience of dying or even companioning the dying is naked and powerful.

LIFE REVIEW or life resolution is a special condition of spiritual transformation. The truth that is acknowledged and the clinging that is released allows the emergence of some noble qualities of our essential nature—love, forgiveness, and gratitude. Life resolution allows a much more vast and spacious perspective, as well as the experience of much more uncongested being. Awareness becomes much less localized, far more inclusive.

This special condition allows the life lived up until that moment to be released. It allows the identification of the self with the story of the life lived to be released. Letting go of the story, and all the snags of the story, we begin to let go of the storyteller. This released attention becomes absorbed in the ease and radiance of present-centered awareness.

No matter how close we are to death, it is not too late to deliberately engage this special condition of awakening. In the apparent midst of life, it is not too early to begin the process of life review.

It is certainly not too early to examine the stories that we have told ourselves about our lives. We can savor what is to be savored with gratitude, forgive what needs to be forgiven with wisdom and compassion, examine what needs to be healed, and focus tender attention on those aspects of our psyche that have remained confused and wounded for so long.

Then we can let it all go—the wounds, the defenses, the stories and the self who told them.

We all have our stories. Most of us have always reacted passively to our stories, as if they were scripts written in stone, as if they were destiny. Most of us have almost always believed them. We've rarely, if ever, questioned them.

We've reacted passively to the contents of our stories as well as to their plot directions. We've identified with the roles assigned in these inner cinemas, and many of us have tried to manage the others in our lives, to subtly and not so subtly attempt to direct them so as to better fit the roles we feel that our stories—of victimhood or entitlement or martyrdom or "alpha-hood"—demand of them.

Most of us have kept the scripts, the subplots and the subtexts, and the hurt and pride of our own narratives to ourselves. We've kept them in a lonely world of our own inner theatre, sitting alone in the dark with old reruns and previews of remarkably similar new releases. We've kept them at a far remove from the present moment and from others.

To do this work of awakening in the last years of our life, our stories are pivotal. We share our stories to gather the courage to attend to our wounds. When the wounds are healed, we can release the stories. With the stories let go, we can stare down the self, now more naked, now thinned, and let go of our attachment to the illusion.

We all have stories that give the self credence. Most of us still carry the wounds that the stories attempt to explain.

The sense of self first arose as a wound, the painful amputation that cut us off into separation. And whatever emotion gave rise to the sense of self so many decades ago—fear or shame or hurt or dissatisfaction—that feeling tone has permeated the ego ever since. It is a theme of most of the self's assumptions, justifications, and habituated patterns.

Ego has been like a street urchin, born of fear and wanting and left to its own devices, guided only by its mistaken understandings. The mistaken understandings are our stories and the self who tells them.

The work of ripening into spiritual maturity, for all of us, is psychospiritual work, and the part of that transformation having to do with the psyche is healing work. Virtually every one of us still has unhealed wounds. We don't go far along the spiritual path before we begin to realize that. For many of us, the pain of the wounds led us to investigate the spiritual path in the first place.

The psyche part of psychospiritual growth has to do with opening to our own vulnerability, with radically accepting our own wounded state. We need to approach this respectfully and mindfully, without judgment or discouragement. We want to approach it with courage. Such courage is engendered in our spiritual practice and strengthened by our committed intention.

We need to respect ourselves enough to know when we're ready. One friend stood at the edge of this examination for a long time, stalled with the question "How can I look at my fear when fear is what I'm afraid of?" She chipped away, employing her courage whenever she gathered it, in accordance with the grace of her intention. She healed her wounds with the recognition of them as painful fictions. With deep insight, she looked into the absence of what she had feared to see.

We want to approach this work on our own psyches with tenderness, humility, and compassion. These are the minds that bring about healing. These are the minds that know that our secret tears connect us to all others. These are the minds that know that the water in our well of sorrow is the same water in everyone's well of sorrow. We can gently hold our intimate weeping as a gift. We can honor it for having led us to melt our walls and falsities. We can begin, finally, to meet with all others out in the open where all is closer to the truth.

We can look at every tender pain, each wound of the fragile psyche, and see that each one led us to this very moment when we can actually see an alternative to living in such a wounded state. Each was a piercing of the paradigm of selfing, each piercing allowing a tiny bit more of the sacred to shine through. Each wound allowed this very moment where we can actually choose to be free from attachment to this small self with all of its pains, where kind teachers from every wisdom tradition shed light on a path of liberation for our benefit.

IT IS WISE and it is liberating to honor the "sacrament of defeat." We begin with acknowledging the need for healing, for weaving the torn pieces of selfing back into wholeness. Sharing, and feeling accepted and seen and understood, by another human being can be very helpful in this healing process. This is the dynamic of many confessional and purification practices. It very often offers a jump-start.

Sharing is healing, or, perhaps more accurately, we allow the beginning of healing when we share our story. Telling the story is pivotal, as it highlights both our wounds and the sense of self that the story explains. In some ways, it seems important that at least one other person on earth hears our story and knows what our experience of existing has been.

Healing can begin in the experience of feeling understood. It could be argued that the experience of being understood is even more nurturing than the experience of feeling loved. In the experience of being understood, we feel known and normalized, even if our story is extraordinary. Each story is an aspect of the human condition. Everyone's story adds deeper insight into our general woundedness and into the ways in which we wound ourselves. We are all vulnerable behind our masks.

Unless we share, we might each stay trapped in our own constructed alienation and separateness, that isolated inner cinema. Understanding from another seems to open a gate into the courage to understand ourselves. When we have the experience of being understood, when someone gives us the gift of attention and simply listens, nonjudgmentally, acceptingly, a shift occurs. This understanding from another seems to allow an opening into ourselves, where the wish to understand and be free is stronger than the wish to hide in isolation and remain contracted.

This liberative practice is a wise one to include in our commitment to awaken in these last years. It is both kind and wise to resolve to allow—in fact, to invite—what has been unmindful to come into and share in mindfulness, to bring the unconsciousness that has directed our lives behind the scenes into the light of consciousness.

Authenticity, greater clarity, and healing occur when we finally see and recognize and open ourselves to our own wounds. We need, with tender mercy and wisdom, to give them the loving attention they have always asked for. Although these wounds are fictions, we suffer within them, just as we can be terrified in the midst of a nightmare.

When we open to our suffering and attend to it for the purpose of this inner healing, healing occurs. Instead of keeping the wounds seemingly tucked away in tightly closed boxes as we've done for so many decades, we simply take a deep breath and begin opening a box or two at a time. Often it's best, if we're just beginning, to start with some boxes that hold the most benign of the wounds.

We simply keep vigil with the wounds, observing them in a mind of wise compassion, no longer dodging away from them or pushing them away. Whatever their feeling tone—fear, shame, hurt, dissatisfaction—we open to them with great lovingkindness. Simply and sanely attended, they can heal.

Healed, we can cohere an ego strong enough, healthy enough, to move beyond itself.

WE CAN SEE the psychological part of our path as wound healing—an important step, as stable growth beyond ego can't occur without a healed foundation. The path goes beyond psychological when we begin to let go of the stories of the wounds. The path enters depths of spirit when we begin to let go of the storyteller of the stories. In a beautiful synergy, the telling of the stories, the healing of the wounds, and the letting go of the stories work together to release the teller of the tales. It is a process that can occur in a microsecond or over years of mindful work. It's a necessary process.

We share the story first as story. Each of us can find a trusted other with whom to do this. We share the story, conscious of it as story, but honest about the fact that we still believe much of it, and that we will continue to, until we have grown considerably in wisdom.

Having the courage to share our story, to stop hiding both from ourselves and others, allows the healing experience of feeling understood and known. It allows connection through our vulnerability. We become spiritual friends, *kalayana mitra* in Sanskrit. We become soul friends, *anam cara* in Gaelic. We encourage each other's boundaries to become more porous in the healing space of undefendedness and acceptance.

Vulnerability not only fosters connection, it fosters compassion. Mirror-neurons dance in deep contentment when such undefended sharing occurs, freeing attention from the dark corners of pain and fear and shame and disappointment. We come into the space of love with each other. We bare our soul.

So we tell our story with compassion for ourselves and for all others who suffer in their stories. We tell it without judgment, although the suffering we've endured with judgment may well be part of our story.

We need wisdom in doing this and a mindfulness developed through practice. As with everything else, our intention makes all the difference. We want to tell the story lightly but thoroughly. We want to see our own stories, witness our own story weaving, for the purpose of recognizing—and then releasing—the habitual thoughts and emotions, the fictions, that have directed the decades of our lives, leaving us in so much limitation and so little freedom.

We don't want to reaffirm the legitimacy of our conclusions or our justifications or our identifications. We don't want to mire our attention more deeply in the beliefs. The point is not to reinvigorate the story or to dwell in the details of it. The point of the storytelling is to open, to share, to take a look at the emotions and wounds and thoughts underlying the story—to hear them all and heal them all and eventually let them all go.

Essentially, we want to see through our stories, to know that it is only in our own imagination and belief that they are carved in stone. We do the work with remembrance that the stories are all fiction, *especially*, as many a Dharma teacher has pointed out, the parts that feel like nonfiction. That's where the deepest wounds are.

THE STORIES THAT we have told ourselves about our lives are carefully edited and there are numerous versions. We could each write a career biography of our lives, a relationship biography, an awakening biography. We could write the story lines of accomplishments and the story lines of failures. Most of us already have, even if we haven't taken the time to clearly articulate these various biographies.

It can be helpful to remember that our stories are determined by our habitual patterns of beliefs and defenses, but they are constructed out of memories. This recognition that our stories arise in the stringing together of memories to create and to conform with a narrative allows us to begin to deconstruct them.

Over these fifty or sixty or seventy years or so, we've each gathered and stored a lot of memories. Our memories are like snapshots, captured bubbles of moments in time, little "episodes" permeated with visuals and with emotions. We string them together in various ways to keep various narratives going. We overlay them on each new moment to give credence to the ongoing illusion of "I."

Almost all of us have prideful narratives containing bubbles of moments of praise and accomplishment and triumph. We can explore how we have strung together this particular narrative. We can ask ourselves which bubbles of memory we've selectively chosen to justify and validate the story of self as filled with praise and accomplishment.

Almost all of us have narratives of shame and guilt and unworthiness, replete with every sharp word and raised eyebrow and the paralyzing self-doubt that blocks all discernment. Again, we can explore how we have strung together this particular narrative as well. We can look at which memories were selectively chosen to justify and validate the story of self as filled with shame and guilt and unworthiness.

We can string together another whole collection of memories for victim narratives. We may have concocted a betrayed narrative or a disappointed or a self-satisfied narrative. How about the imposter story or the avenger story? Do we have accounting stories of who owes us what or regret stories of all the chances we were afraid to take? Do we have "good" stories? What would be our own lame version of Annie Dillard's sobering phrase: "I kept a tidy house. I made my own cheese balls."

We can look. There's much to learn about the dynamics of being stuck, about the dynamics of suffering, by looking. It is both wise and kind to set aside time to do so. We hold the intention to eventually experience each new moment with clear seeing, without distortion.

Out of a million memories, we select the ones that support and validate whatever narrative is holding sway. For every thousand memories we carefully select, we forget that there are hundreds of thousands of other memories that don't substantiate the narrative in any way at all. We use selective vision, selective memory, in the creation and maintenance of the stories we have been using to explain and underpin and understand and justify ourselves. We watch politicians do this all the time, spinning factoids to serve their own purposes. It takes courage and humility and honesty to acknowledge that we do this all the time, as well. We have lived in "inappropriate attention," attention that unexaminedly adheres to our beliefs, attention without wisdom, without clear seeing.

We pick and choose our memories and string them together so as to keep the stories coherent, to maintain our paradigms. We need to grow in the clarity of our recognition that our own mind fabricated the stories that the strung-together memories seem to substantiate. We also need to grow in the clarity of our recognition that our own mind fabricated the memories themselves.

> An ignorant mind,
> If stirred by thought,
> Turns the formless into a solid entity.
>
> —Saraha

We can choose, in the still mind of meditation, to simply let go. When we let go of the story, we free the memories, and we free ourselves. We free the memories, and they simply dissipate into empty space. They are unrelated. They do not form a narrative. Released, these memories will no longer trap us in their imaginings. Released, they harm no one, since they were only always our own mental creations, not entities at all.

In the still mind of meditation, we will come to see that the string that held it all together was our own mistaken conception that there is a continuously abiding, unchanging "me." We need to ask ourselves, what is this "I"? What is its nature? That "me to which all of these events happened" is an illusion. We imputed "I" upon the toddler that we were, the adolescent, the young adult, and the adult at midlife.

We impute "I" upon this senior citizen now. What thoughts continue to stir it into a solid entity, a tense, seemingly continuous congestion?

We would do well to ask ourselves: what is the compulsion to impute "I" anew upon every arising moment? The "I" impulse so rapidly asserts itself, showering "I" onto each next moment, like an automatic weapon shattering each arising's freshness. It is enormously helpful to look for and become mindful of this impulse, the unnecessary and burdensome intrusion of selfing.

As we continue with the work of life resolution, we let go of all of the stories that we have held about our "past." We can begin to see how we use the present merely as a place to project a "future" for the self and its repetitive narrative, as a Band-Aid to hold together past and future. Doing so, we miss Presence.

Gradually, our awakening stance will transform from congested "me"—always missing the present, to mindful witnessing of that continuing tendency, and—finally—to simple being, here and now, with no need to add either story or storyteller. No Dharma lag at all.

It can be helpful to let ourselves imagine what it would be like to be at ease with the continuous flow of rising and falling. What would life be like without the compulsion to create a story, without the compulsion to defend and grasp and explain? What would my experience of life be, were self-reference with its Medusa's head of potential snags to simply fade into the sunset? Such imagining can inspire us.

"Kindsight" is a beautiful word that describes the wisest approach to this work of releasing attention's entanglement in our own narratives, this often stumbling and chaotic part of our path. Kindsight allows us to open into places in our heart where we were previously afraid to go. With kindsight, we heal. Healed, we let go. We surrender. Surrendering, letting go, we are just as we are. That is transcendence.

Our growing, simple awareness of being allows us, increasingly, to simply be.

> Finally I am coming to the conclusion
> that my highest ambition is to be what I already am.
> That I will never fulfill my obligation to surpass myself unless
> I first accept myself,
> and if I accept myself fully in the right way,
> I will already have surpassed myself.
>
> —THOMAS MERTON

This is the beautiful process in which we can engage in these last years of our lives, if we wish. It is a process of lightening. Perhaps we fall and stumble, perhaps we at times become discouraged, perhaps at times it's painful, but persevering in our intention and with our compassion, we continue to become lighter in every way.

We become lighter in terms of lessening the weight of all of our baggage. We lighten the load of personhood. We become lighter as less and less congested energy of old patterns and beliefs obscures the radiance of formless awareness shining through form. We can become, as Dharma teacher Reginald Ray says, "ablaze with wakefulness."

> It is a wonderful day in a life
> when one is finally able to stand
> before the long, deep mirror of one's own reflection
>   and view oneself
> with appreciation, acceptance, and forgiveness.
> On that day
> one breaks through the falsity of images and expectations
> which have blinded one's spirit.
> One can only learn to see who one is
> when one learns to view oneself
> with the most intimate and forgiving
> compassion.
>
> —John O'Donohue

Before healing, it is profoundly unwise to think or to say, "This is just the way I am." It is a complacency that will keep us from looking and letting go and growing. What that phrase really means, prior to the work of mindful growth, is "This is the way I believe I am, this is who I think is me, and I'm too lazy or scared to look any deeper, to see if what I've assumed and believed all this time is true."

Paradoxically, as with many things on the spiritual path, after we have done the work of releasing attachment to our wounds and stories and roles and beliefs and striving, "this is just the way I am" is a lovely and affirming statement of truth. No beliefs, just being, pure and simple and unselfconscious. It is a balanced state of acceptance, with healthy pride and healthy humility, grateful ownership.

We may wonder who we would be without the story. We may wonder what is left when we're free from habits. We may wonder what we will lose. We may wonder if we will become invisible or bland or simply empty space when we are free from selfing. We may wonder if we will be an easy target.

We will not be boring without our posturing. We will not be unseen. We will not be tense. We will reside in greater peace and share with more generous hearts. We will rest in more stable strength in the midst of anguish. We will have more joyful and relaxed fearlessness and be far more able and happy to live in mystery and awe. We will have more compassion and more skill to pull ourselves up again when we fall back into the dream of self.

It's most likely that we won't be levitating around as bejeweled buddhas. We shouldn't count on walking through our neighborhoods with white robes and a halo, perpetually holding a lamb or some other small creature with straw on it.

Our presence, though, will be a powerful energy field—no doormat at all. The power of our presence will be offerable, available with great generosity of spirit, to a world that not only needs more goodness and wisdom but needs affirmation that such simple goodness and wisdom is attainable by all of us totally ordinary beings.

One friend, committing himself to using these last years wisely and meaningfully, said the wish arose from seeing so much suffering in himself and in the world that he wanted "to be an example of another way to live." He wanted to become "a being that can actually be a comfort and a guide."

Gentleness arises in this undefended openness, in this presence without the armor or the obstruction of story. Continuing to practice, we will find in ourselves the courage to be gentle with our vulnerability and the vulnerability of all others. It takes heroic humility to be ourselves.

Letting go of the story and our attachment to selfing, we can finally stand in the strength of defenselessness. That defenselessness arises in wisdom and abides as compassion.

We will be, unselfconsciously, the perfectly unique, never-to-be-replicated human beings we are. Only at ease. Only sharing the ease.

It will be our flowering and our fruition, and we will look no different, except maybe more relaxed. Our flowering and fruition will leave us softened and sweetened, more permeable, more free, and more able to care about ourselves, others, and our planet.

Our presence will matter more and more as we engage in awakening. Our presence will increasingly bring wholesomeness and wholeness and holiness into the world. We will be a balm and a bridge and a light and there will be a great joy in serving in those ways.

We can experience, in this very life and in these very years, the grace in aging. We can be ready for the time of our death, having made this life profoundly meaningful. Having developed the capacity to be present, we can enter the next moment more lightly, present within the great mystery as it continues to unfold in its endlessly changing display.

Letting go of our attachment to wounds and to memories, to stories and to selfing, we will have faced the first death: the death of ego.

Saint Francis—one who did love animals who were covered with straw but never demanded that we all carry one around—said that if we face the first death, the second death, the death of the temporarily appearing body, can do no harm.

OPENING THE HEART AND OPENING THE MIND

> We still
> and always want waking.
>
> —Annie Dillard

Although the death of another being can be a time of awe and profundity and even beauty, it is very difficult to be present and to stay present, without shutting down.

Although the process of our own dying can be a time of profound spiritual transformation, it can also be difficult beyond imagining.

To be truthful, it is difficult, also, to be alive. Being a person is no easy thing. It takes courage.

Each of the three—the death of another, our own death, and our experience of life—is an unfolding that is both beautiful and terrible. The difficulty, the suffering, experienced in each arises from our own tense, tight grasping to an "I" whose heart is less than opened and whose mind is well-defended. The opening of the heart and the opening of the mind are the two fundamental tasks of both living and dying. These openings lead directly to the experience of union with the ground of being, always already so.

By the time we've reached our later decades, we've had a long haul of mindlessness, of sleepwalking. Almost every last one of us has experienced moments with an awful sense of being trapped in smallness and confusion, fearful of all we do not wish to see. That which is "difficult to face" in a human life is given as an alternative definition of *dukkha,* most often translated as suffering, by Buddhist teacher Mark Epstein.

> Hold me against the dark: I am afraid.
> Circle me with your arms. I am made
> So tiny and my atoms so unstable
> That at any moment I may explode. I am unable
> To contain myself in unity. My outlines shiver
> With the shock of living.
>
> —Madeleine L'Engle

There *is* a shock of living. We *are* tiny in a self. Our atoms *are* unstable; at any moment we may explode. Selfing is precarious business. It has no ground. The best it can hope for is Band-Aids—and temporary ones at that.

And there *is* a shock of dying. Our outlines, as we conceive of them, shiver. We have closed our hearts to avoid feeling just such fear. We have spent decades deluded into thinking that, in the deep, closed-off recesses of self, we might be safe.

One of the most meaningful things that often happens as a terminally ill person dies can best be described as "the opening of the heart." This opening of the heart is another of the special conditions of the transformative process of dying that we would do well to incorporate into our lives far before the moment of death.

The opening of the heart is a radical release of all that doesn't matter—of all that has always kept our heart closed. When our heart opens, we lose nothing. Nothing that can be lost is real. As we die and the heart opens, we are no longer, in Nisargadatta's piercing phrase, "burdened with a person."

To cultivate an open heart in the midst of life is a noble aspiration and an immeasurably rewarding one. We open our hearts when hiding becomes more unbearable than letting go. Opening our heart is a deep surrender of the burden of being someone.

We can effect this transformation in the midst of these last years, if we so wish. The opening of the heart is a liberation from the limitations of fear. Opening the heart dissolves the wall between our self and others and dissolves the wall between our self and the sacred. It leaves the heart with no need to defend. Without self-reference, there is no separation. Without separation, there is no fear. Without fear, the confinement of defendedness, a strategy based on misconception, is recognized as draining and unnecessary.

In peace, we disarm. In strength, we have no need for props or positions. In goodness, we have no need to harm. Our only needs are to grow in clarity and to grow in generosity. We want to cultivate an undefended mind and an undefended heart. Defenselessness is a beautiful state of being, one which we would do well to intend for ourselves and to wish for all others.

Opening our heart, life becomes not so much about difficulty, although difficulties may certainly still arise for us. We simply, with an open heart, hold everything more lightly. We hold everything, in healer Barbara Brennan's beautiful phrase, "only lightly dusted with form."

We can ask ourselves questions. Inquiry helps us to stay on track, to not get so lost in the small distractions, swept away in any kind of busy-ness or upset or one more fantasy posing as real. What shift can I make in this moment to live any more lightly? With more ease? With more gratitude? More peace? How can I shift my view, right now, into a kinder heart?

Imagine the experience of simply being, without resistance or snags or enmeshment.

When difficulties arise, we see exactly where we need to grow. Having an open heart allows us to keep to the task with great and sweet tenderness. One friend used the time left to her with her short prognosis to clear self out of the way so that she could experience, as she put it, "Being being." She wanted to experience love loving and clarity illuminating. A few days from her death, she shared that "the brightness just deepens."

There is much to learn by observing where we still cling to staying closed, much to learn from observing how and from whom we withhold our warmth. There is great healing to be had when we attend to our resistances and defenses. It is more than worth the effort to set aside time periodically to check on "the state of the heart," to deliberately relax whatever tightness or exclusivity remains within it. Ultimately, our own peace resides in loving all beings without exception.

To cultivate an open heart, as this dying friend did, is to allow ourselves to experience the rush of freedom from fear and the absolute glory of being able to love, fully and completely and wholeheartedly. We know what joy and richness we've experienced with loved ones. Imagine being in love with everyone, being in love with it all, the radiant gaze of love never faltering. This effortless loving is our essential nature, the power of the formless that appears us. The more we allow our heart to open, to simply be, soft and resting in natural sweetness and loveliness, the more we enter into awareness beyond self, beyond form only. Opening the heart brings us to our shimmering home in communion.

To allow the noble qualities to flourish in us and pour forth through us, we can engage in the practices of the noble qualities.

It is within the capacity of each of us to realize our own essential nature and embody these signs and indications of awakening and the awakened state.

It is possible, with intention and practice and grace, for each of us to cultivate the minds that pull attention out of the mental poisons, the afflictive mindstates of greed and aversion, in all of their disguises. They lurk in the dark and primitive recesses of our brains, toxically firing away, keeping us asleep. The noble states of mind rewire these neural pathways, pulling them out into the kindness mindfulness makes way for.

The practice of the Four Immeasurables, the *brahmaviharas* of Buddhism, is such a practice. This practice cultivates the minds of love, compassion, joy, and equanimity.

In this practice, love is seen, simply and elegantly, without the confusions of grasping, as the wish for all beings to be happy and, especially, to be as fulfilled in their longing for the sacred as we wish for ourselves. Every being, without exception.

A simple practice, on the cushion or off, is to generate the experience of "being in love." Although we may use the mental image of our own precious child or our own dearest lover to generate the feeling at first, we can quickly dissolve the mental image of the face we pinned on the feeling. We can own our own capacity to love and dispense with the prompt. Then we take that open-hearted, "in love" mind and greet each arising moment with it. Over time and with practice, we cultivate the beautiful mind of lovingkindness, extending it with increasing depth and inclusivity and spontaneity as our hearts open into their own boundless and natural generosity.

In the practice of the Four Immeasurables, compassion is seen as the wish that all beings, including ourselves, be free from suffering. We begin to recognize pain as pain regardless of who appears to be experiencing it. We practice opening our hearts as a mother opens to give birth, in successive waves of opening, each wave increasingly able to unflinchingly hold the sorrow in all around us.

> When I think about the sadness of the people in this world,
> their sadness becomes mine.
>
> . . . .
>
> O that my priest's robe were wide enough to gather up
> all the suffering people
> in this floating world.
>
> —RYOKAN

The great compassion expressed by Ryokan is called, in contemplative Christian tradition, the "imitation of Christ." Deepened capacity for compassion is present in every wisdom lineage, in every transformative moment of living and dying. Willing to look, we see sorrow. Seeing sorrow, our cold indifference and defenses melt in open compassion.

In the practice of the Four Immeasurables, joy is cultivated and delighted in, whether the experience is one we have or one we observe in another. Wherever it is found, joy is cultivated and responded to sympathetically, resonantly. True joy is scarce. Shared joy is more scarce. Once the beautiful mind of joy is cultivated, arising independently of circumstances, the heart-felt wish arises for all beings to exist within this beautiful mind.

In this practice, equanimity is cultivated through the practice of the other three minds. Equanimity announces itself as a mind free from self-reference and, therefore, free from reactivity. It is a balanced mind. Free from grasping and aversion, it rests, at ease. Without self-reference, it simply *is*, with natural great peace. It is a heart that is fully open. It is a refuge and, like all refuges, it is open to receiving those who wish to enter and open to sharing with all around.

The practice of the Four Immeasurables cultivates those beautiful heartminds in a way that is thoroughly inclusive, so that each of the four—wishing love, offering compassion, sharing joy, and holding and extending equanimity—encompasses all beings, includes all arisings, omitting no one and nothing. The generation and cultivation of those minds, as they become increasingly more spontaneous and continuous, releases attention previously trapped in selfing into awareness that is pristine and uncongested.

To cultivate any of the minds of the Four Immeasurables, and hold to it, remaining unwaveringly within that awareness, is called a "sublime abiding." The sublime abidings are always only a breath away, once having become familiar with them. They always offer entry into our deepest, most beautiful, and most essential self.

Christian contemplative practice offers doors to the sublime abodes as well; David Steindl-Rast, the beloved Catholic monk, paints the word "gratitude" on his. Thomas Keating, the Catholic contemplative who resurrected centering prayer from medieval obscurity, names stillness as one of his gateless gates. Richard Rohr points us to courageous presence.

The energy of the love we generate and the love through which we live and move and have our being, the love that is inherent in ever-present awareness beyond self, is identical. Generating the mind of love, for example, we enter love. We enter a more refined and rarified, subtle awareness. We enter the love that has been here all the time anyway, just waiting for us to show up.

This is true of any of the noble minds, all of the sublime abidings. They are vehicles of release from the experience of life as form only, as exclusively self. Generating joy, we enter and offer joy. Generating peace, we enter and offer peace. Generating stillness, we enter and offer equanimity. Generating any of the noble minds, we enter the realms of the formless, the ground of being, the matrix of every noble quality.

Any cultivation of a noble mind, any experience of it, is grace. Our hearts open in grace. Experiencing grace, we can no longer find any reason to keep our hearts closed.

ANOTHER BEAUTIFUL OCCURRENCE often happens as a person dies. It, also, is one of the special conditions of any transformative process. It could well be called "the opening of the mind." The opening of the mind is an essential task for any of us who wishes to awaken.

As we die, we will come face to face with the uncertainty of impermanence. Dying, we must choicelessly confront the mystery underlying and manifesting all appearance, as well as our own impotence before it. The process of dying forces us to recognize not-knowing, forces us to stand in mystery, eventually free from the scrambling need to know, eventually at ease in not-knowing.

As we age, we increasingly become aware of impermanence. We can begin to recognize the new mystery of each moment if we look. We can begin to let go of our fear of looking as we engage in awakening.

In the face of mystery, the paltriness and some of the absurdity of what we think we know and what we believe is starkly revealed. Penetrating experiences of insight allow us to clearly recognize that our ignorance has always led us in the wrong direction.

As we practice, we begin to directly see, with increasingly clarity, that who we think ourselves to be exists as a concept. Ego exists in a state of ignorance.

Self has always settled for the false refuge of conceptual knowing. Self has always been convinced of the assumption that our conceptual knowing defines and captures reality. We cling to the concept of self and to the conceptual universe selfing creates.

We cling, with fingers crossed, hoping beyond hope that there may be nouns where in truth there are only verbs. We are fixed in our predilection for nouns that we can grasp or blame. We infinitely prefer nouns to fleeting, ungraspable verbs. With our nouns, the "knowns" of our thoughts, assumptions, paradigms, and beliefs, we are pulled out of alignment in the simple truth of the present moment. Bare witnessing gets bent and distorted in conceptuality's pull in much the same way as an object that we know to be straight appears curved when viewed from under water.

Each of us has the capacity for liberation from interpreted perceptions, deeply believed biographical narratives, tightly held paradigms, and an erroneously fixed relationship with each moment's new arising. The capacity for liberation ripens by engaging in a practice of not-knowing, of cultivating ease with not-knowing. This is an open stance of being, an undefended mind. We can, with courage and practice and maybe even a bit of disenchanted world-weariness come to the place of readiness where we can approach mystery, can open to inquiry without agenda, to bare and curious and naked attention.

If we so intend and so practice, we can, in the midst of life, in this time of our aging, allow our mind to open. We simply sit and look. We will, in fairly short order, become aware of the convincing fictions that we have imputed upon simple neural firings. We will come to see through the fictions, clearing the air of their noise, removing the veils they place before the innocence of clear awareness.

We will find that there is a lot of "knowing" to shed. Saint Augustine called it "learned ignorance." Truth be told, however invested we are in our own thoughts and feelings and attitudes and beliefs, we really don't know much of anything at all beyond the logistics of navigating the appearance of a world agreed to in our consensus.

A few years back, someone created a wonderful slide show called "Powers of Ten." It began with a view of endless space, vast expanses of void dotted with infinite points of light. Zooming in by the power of ten, the next view was one of luminous galaxies, stars without number seeming to create a solidity of light, shifting like a murmuration of white starlings. Zooming in again by the power of ten, our own galaxy, the Milky Way, a broad and shimmering avenue of light. Several zooms more and there appeared our beautiful green and blue and white planet. With another zoom to the power of ten could be seen the unmistakable peninsula of Florida. Again a zoom to Tallahassee. Another zoom brought into view an observatory in Tallahassee. Zooming in by the power of ten again, a tree behind the observatory was revealed. Again a zoom to a leaf on the tree, labeled in the slide show "actual leaf." More zooms brought the view to the cells of the leaf and the atoms of the cells of the leaf until the final zoom by the power of ten brought the view of endless space, vast expanses of void dotted with infinite points of light, exactly as in the beginning.

"Actual leaf." Each "actual leaf" is only our own imputation on a momentary movement of the ground of being. It has functional value, to be sure. We watch its fresh green arising in the spring and rake it in the fall, breathing in its oxygen all summer. But "actual leaf" is a fraction of the holy panoramic mystery of impermanence and interbeing giving rise to its appearance.

We make "actual leaves" everywhere. We make, with our imputation, an "actual object of aversion." We make, with our imputation, an "actual object of desire." And at the bottom of it all, at the bottom of all desire and aversion, we make, with our imputation, an "actual me."

We have taken the functional value of our words and concepts as the full extent of what is. We collapse vastness and wonder. Instead of recognizing the holiness in the mundane, we collapse holiness to the level of the mundane.

Every time we label with a single word, we impute an entire cosmos in which that word and all of its implications, utterly interrelated, exist. We impute an entire cosmos in which the "I" doing the labeling, and all that the thought "I" implies, exist. Every concept is, in the end, self-referential.

"I" unfolds a universe. "I" also collapses a universe unto itself.

Clinging to self-reference, clinging to the stories that seem to support the self-reference, we are like a physicist engaged in the most subtle measurement of form. We collapse the potentiality, including the potentiality to awaken, of each moment.

We need labels and concepts to function in the world effectively, but it is wise to use them lightly, mindfully. Although we have thought of the conceptual mind as always of use, like a universal remote, it is a blessing to see its limitations.

WHAT WE NEED if we intend to spiritually ripen, what will help us become elders, is to question everything. It is kind and wise to question our every tacit assumption, so predisposed to impose its view on each new moment.

Our instinct to question everything was once active, alive and well, in each of us. For many of us, that was our generation's cry and one of our gifts to future generations. We need to question our own assumptions. We need to question the authority we have handed over to those assumptions.

We each have a natural curiosity. Complacency, our desire for comfort, and selfing's countless other needs have pushed our natural curiosity far into the background. One friend, turning seventy, had a powerful insight into the consequences of her own resistance to naked inquiry. "If I stay as a strong comfort seeker," she said, "I'll sink."

We haven't lost our natural curiosity, our capacity to explore the arising of each and every moment with innocence and without attachment or preconception, without self-reference. It's retrievable. We just need to dust it off.

WE MAY BE AWARE of ordinary mind's tendency to "fill in the blanks" of an observation, to normalize and attempt to make sense of it. We quickly read neon signs with letters missing, for example, or jump to a conclusion with sparse evidence. We impute "body" on a thousand disparate, fleeting sensations. The separate sense of self has a deeply entrenched habit pattern of quickly seeking order, quickly feeling that we understand. Without mindfulness, this pattern remains unconscious. We don't often stop to go so deeply into a moment's experience that we see, that we directly know, the way it is. Just this. As it is. Unadorned.

Our tendency is to quickly grasp notions like formlessness and mystery and impermanence with conceptual minds, to feel that we "know" them through the quick grasp. The quick grasp allows no contemplation, no transformation. It leaves us untouched. It leaves us not dazzled by the emptiness of space, not humbled by boundaryless vastness, not made more real, vulnerable, and gratefully appreciative with the recognition of our own fleeting existence.

Two thousand years ago, Jesus told us to love one another. He was giving us the key to our own holy awareness beyond self. He was telling us exactly how to become liberated, how to awaken. He was giving us the simplest possible key.

Three words. Love. One. Another. Love one another. We can quickly understand each one of the words. We can quickly understand the sentence. Conceptually.

If we actually took the words into our hearts and understood them nonconceptually, with open minds, through naked inquiry and the direct experience of their meaning, and applied that understanding and embodied it, the experience of life on this planet would be radically different. If we embodied the nonconceptual understanding of those three words, "love one another," in every moment of our lives, we would all already be the buddhas Jesus wished for us to be.

People who've had any experience below the surface of appearances and beyond the fictions of stories know that they don't know. It is humbling to stand before mystery. Richard Rohr observes that we end up standing in awe before it, in wonder at eternity and depth and, as he says, "a love which is incomprehensible to the mind." Awe-inspiring. Filled with wonder. But also experienceable, directly knowable as the very depth of being.

> It is the nothing, the Mystery, the Emptiness alone
> that needs to be realized:
> not known but felt, not thought but breathed,
> not an object but an atmosphere.
>
> —Ken Wilber

The great wisdom traditions invite us into openness, into open mind. Their call responds to our yearning, a yearning we have all known, for the joy of release from the smallness of beliefs, for awe, for mystery. Einstein fell in love with mystery. Jianzhi Sengcan, the Third Chinese Patriarch of Zen, disappeared into it and awakened.

To be dazzled with mystery, unhindered by the weight of knowns and the inflexible tensions of knowing, we need to let go of what we think we know. We can let go of the convictions we've held for so long and the stories with which we've lulled ourselves to sleep. We can let go of our judgments and our biases that have kept equanimity waiting at the door for decades. We open our mind by letting go of all that has filled it.

This letting go is a bit like cleaning out a house in which we have lived for a long time, in preparation for a move to a much smaller home. We can pack up many a box and get it ready for Goodwill or the sidewalk without a second thought as to its contents. These are like the thoughts that, although we've held them for decades, upon examination we find are quite easy to discard. And, then, once in a while, we'll find an object or a thought to which sentimentality, for example, or fear or anger or pride, has attached and we watch ourselves clutching it a bit tightly, unable quite yet to put it in the discard box.

It is instructive to watch where our resistances are to this letting go. Our resistances highlight where we're stuck, where peace and equanimity and wisdom are blocked. They highlight the stories that still fill our minds, the stories whose release would free us. It helps to ask ourselves—often—what beliefs do I still believe? What unexamined assumptions remain? Where do I cling to "being right" and to thinking I know? What keeps me from inquiring with a stance of naked curiosity? What am I afraid of? Where do I not want to look?

Who is looking? In what awareness is that "who"? What is the nature of that awareness? Is there a "who" who can own awareness? Is it ownable?

It helps to ask the questions repeatedly, like a sentry under orders to ask for papers no matter how familiar the visitor. The practice of not-knowing, of open mind, involves making the familiar unfamiliar.

To not thoroughly question our beliefs and assumptions about self, to ignore what we can potentially learn by simply looking at the nature of mind, is foolish. We want to thoroughly explore, without preconception, the constant concept churning that has kept us in ignorance.

Ignorance will not help us in the time we have remaining. It will not help with aging and all of its predictable sufferings. It will not help with dying. The ignorance of the ego will bear no witness to anyone about anything except the cowardice and the blind and uncaring persistence of self-grasping. The ego exists in a dream state. It doesn't care about awakening. It's like a teenager who only wants to sleep.

Gil Fronsdale, a respected American Dharma teacher, suggests that we add the statement "I don't know" after every thought. Incorporating such a simple practice breaches selfing's defended walls, opening space within our tightly held paradigms. We can begin to allow ourselves to hold our thoughts more lightly and to move beyond the limitations of our oceans of belief, the sea of facts in which we've been so stressed and lost, endlessly treading water.

> Do you think I know what I am doing?
> That for one breath or half-breath I belong to myself?
> As much as a pen knows what it's writing,
> or the ball can guess where it's going next.
> —RUMI

Not-knowing is a stillness. That stillness arises in a surrender of the chronic tension of our survival-based need to know, arises from a growing willingness to simply experience, to simply explore.

Not-knowing is fearful and unsettling at first. Jeff Foster calls it "a free fall into mystery." It is a gate to awareness beyond conception, beyond form, beyond self. To know that we don't know and to allow our awareness to relax deeply into a mind of open inquiry is to access depths of insight and wisdom far more meaningful and profound and true than anything we can access in conceptual knowing. We arrive, undefended by conception, at the holy ground of being. We can, in Einstein's words, stand like curious children before the great mystery.

To open our mind is to soften its crystallizations, melt its densities, allow the energy of attention to release out of congestion and into awareness and merge with it, abiding tranquilly. When the mind opens, the mind calms. There is less to stir it into a choppy sea. It becomes more serene, therefore, more mirror-like, more reflective of the truth of things. Buddhist wisdom speaks, in piercing insight, of naked awareness as emptiness's reflection.

This innocence of inquiry generously allows us all to free ourselves of the tightly held concepts and beliefs that obscure realization.

The opening of the mind is a liberation from distractions, a liberation from fictions and beliefs, a liberation from any fixed position. It signals the beginning of the end of ignorance, the awakening from the dream of self. We, as we allow ourselves to awaken, having applied wise effort and having abided in wise intention, can experience a liberation from the ignorance that sees the impermanent as permanent, that sees tension as contentment, that sees the inessential as essential, and that sees self as inherently existing.

This awakening awareness is revealed as a "nondwelling space," free from reference, free from attachment to a localized sense of self. It is free in every way. It is always and already freely available to us. We simply have to earn, through practice and intention, the capacity to abide in it. We have to develop the capacity to discover it. We have to, through surrender, let go into the divine flow.

THE CALLING CARD of wisdom, its signature, is compassion. We will know that we have grown in some wisdom when our compassion becomes more genuine and spontaneous and continuous. Compassion is alpha and omega on this noble path. It is our beginning point and our forever point. It is where sorrow and peace, vulnerability and strength, meet. As His Holiness the Dalai Lama so beautifully and simply puts it, "my religion is kindness."

> Before you know kindness as the deepest thing inside,
> you must know sorrow as the other deepest thing.
> You must wake up with sorrow.
> You must speak to it till your voice
> catches the thread of all sorrows
> and you see the size of the cloth.
>
> Then it is only kindness that makes sense anymore,
> only kindness that ties your shoes

and sends you out into the day to mail letters and purchase
bread,
only kindness that raises its head
from the crowd of the world to say
it is I you have been looking for,
and then goes with you everywhere
like a shadow or a friend.

—Naomi Shihab Nye

As compassion and wisdom begin to come into fruition, we begin to realize the boundlessness of the heart's clarity. May we all daily grow until we know and embody these boundless states. May we all calmly abide in the equanimity of these boundless states.

Until we do so, may we all take refuge each day in *buddha*, the awakened state of utterly purified goodness. May we all take refuge each day in *dharma*, the utterly clear wisdom of truth. May we all take refuge each day in *sangha*, the utterly beloved beauty of interbeing. We can do that no matter our spiritual path. Buddha, dharma, and sangha are refuge, the three jewels of any practice.

Buddha simply means awakened awareness, awareness resting in ultimate reality, the one. *Sangha* is simply the utterly interdependent appearances of all of us, the many. *Dharma* is the truth that mediates between buddha and sangha. *Dharma* holds the seeming paradox of the two, the conditioned and the unconditioned, form and formless, in one taste, all sacred.

May we each move closer each day to becoming refuge ourselves, to embodying the shimmering jewels of practice.

May this last chapter of our lives find us all gravitating toward the holy, moving closer to home and bringing home closer to all we encounter.

Rather than viewing old age and death as an ignoble and undignified end, we can offer a view of these last years as an opportunity, gracefully offered and gratefully taken, to meet and embody our noble and dignified purpose and, then, to offer its fruition.

We can give a different sense of what these last years can be in a human life, offering an example for our children and our grandchildren, for each other's children and grandchildren. We can bring light into our benighted culture, so far lost down grasping's long detour, and bring healing to our precious and beautiful planet, so harmed by the ignorance of the unawakened state.

AFTERWORD

A SPIRITUAL INVENTORY

> If you want to identify me,
> ask me not where I live,
> or what I like to eat,
> or how I comb my hair,
> but ask me what I am living for, in detail,
> ask me what I think is keeping me from living fully
> for the thing I want to live for.
>
> —THOMAS MERTON

TO AWAKEN IN THE TIME afforded us, it is helpful to do a periodic inventory of where we are. It's not so much an inventory of how many times we've practiced or how many retreats or pujas or novenas we've done, not a question of how many rosaries or mantras we've said or teachings we've listened to, although all of these practices can have their place.

We want to periodically look at where we have ripened and gratefully own that. We want to look at where we resist ripening, where we still hold back, and earnestly engage more of our being in the effort to ripen. Christian wisdom observes, "By their fruits ye shall know them." We can look at how we're doing.

Any bit of goodness and wisdom and love and compassion that we grow, however tiny, is an immeasurable gift to ourselves and to an endless universe. Every tiny bit. And with every bit more of goodness and wisdom and love and compassion, the universe smiles with delight, just as a parent would as the beloved toddler learns to walk.

> Monk: "What is the essence of your practice?"
> Basho: "Whatever is needed."

What do I need to clear up or let go of to be more peaceful?

What are my resistances to vulnerability?

What are my resistances to being fully present?

What are my distractions?

What are my fears?

How thorough is my forgiveness of others?

How thorough is my forgiveness of myself?

How deep is my gratitude?

How generous is my heart?

How honest is my self-inquiry? Where do I not want to look?

Where do I hold back from love?

How easy am I able to be with any kind of unease, disappointment, pain, suffering?

What are my aversions?

Where do I cling?

Where do I limit my identity?

How have I nurtured patience, with myself and others?

How spontaneous is my compassion, with myself and others?

Am I ready to set aside judging?

What are the stories I still tell myself?

How harmless am I?

What helps me experience the presence of spirit?

What keeps me from living in that presence?

APPENDIX

A QUESTIONNAIRE ON AGING

1. What is your age?

2. How do you feel about aging?

    - How has your appearance changed?
      How do you feel about it?

    - How has your position in the world changed?
      How do you feel about it?

- How has your reception in the world changed?
  How do you feel about it?

- How have your perceptions about yourself changed?
  How do you feel about it?

3. Have your values changed as you have aged? Which values have been discarded? Which have been consciously chosen and retained? What are your emerging values?

4. What are your fears about your own experience of aging—to date and in the future?

5. What views about aging and the elderly—both positive and negative—have you absorbed from your cultural and family background, and how do you feel these may be unconsciously influencing your current thoughts, feelings, beliefs, and attitudes? In what ways have you deliberately tried to counter any of these background attitudes that you feel are negative or unhelpful?

6. As you consider your inner life—your general state of ease or unease—what still needs healing? Are there habit patterns of thoughts and feelings, perhaps left over from decades ago, that still cause stress? Do you see it as possible to work through these obstructions? What are you doing to release any remaining, persistent habit patterns so as to spend the rest of your life in a mind that is more peaceful and at ease?

7. In which aspects of living have you most directed your attention and energy to date? What has been nurturing, fulfilling, supportive? What has been stressful for you?

8. How do you intend to direct your attention and energy in the years remaining to you?

9. What losses have you faced? What losses do still you face? How do you cope with loss? What would help you cultivate the capacity to better handle inevitable loss, to maintain a relationship of greater ease with impermanence?

10. What are your thoughts about your death? What inner strengths are you developing or do you wish to work on developing so as to face sickness, aging, and death with greater peace and equanimity?

11. What are your thoughts about spiritual maturity? What is your commitment to your own spiritual maturity? What steps have you taken? What steps do you intend to take? What keeps you from taking them now?

CITATIONS

Excerpt from "Lost" from *Traveling Light: Collected and New Poems*, copyright © 1999 by David Wagoner. Used with permission of the poet and the University of Illinois Press.

"Hitch Haiku" by Gary Snyder, from *The Back Country*, copyright © 1968 by Gary Snyder. Reprinted by permission of New Directions Publishing Corporation.

Excerpt from "Instruments (2)" from *The Ordering of Love* by Madeleine L'Engle. Shaw Books.

Excerpt from "Keeping Quiet" from *Extravagaria* by Pablo Neruda, translated by Alastair Reid. Translation copyright © 1974 by Alastair Reid. Reprinted by permission of Farrar, Straus, and Giroux, LLC.

Excerpts from "Blessing in the Chaos," copyright © Jan L. Richardson at janrichardson.com.

INDEX

Page numbers followed by "q" indicate quotations.

D

E

F

I

M

N

ABOUT THE AUTHOR

KATHLEEN DOWLING SINGH was a Dharma practitioner, mentor, and in-demand speaker and teacher. She's the author of *The Grace in Dying: How We Are Transformed Spiritually As We Die; The Grace in Living: Recognize It, Trust It, Abide in It;* and *Unbinding: The Grace Beyond Self*. Kathleen died in 2017.

WHAT TO READ NEXT FROM WISDOM

GRACE IN LIVING

Recognize It, Trust It, Abide in It

Kathleen Dowling Singh

"This is an instruction manual on opening our heart to a life that is richer, more meaningful, and joyful. It is difficult to imagine that anyone would not benefit from this luminous book."
—Larry Dossey, MD, author of *One Mind*

LIVING AND DYING WITH CONFIDENCE

A Day-by-Day Guide

Anyen Rinpoche and Allison Choying Zangmo

"Anyen Rinpoche has skillfully woven the Dharma teachings into these everyday contemplations on death, which will be very beneficial, especially for those in denial or dealing with loss."
—Tenzin Palmo, founder of Dongyu Gatsal Ling Nunnery

HOW TO BE SICK

A Buddhist-Inspired Guide for the Chronically Ill and Their Caregivers

Toni Bernhard, foreword by Sylvia Boorstein

"Full of hopefulness and promise . . . this book is a perfect blend of inspiration and encouragement. Toni's engaging teaching style shares traditional Buddhist wisdom in a format that is accessible to all readers."
—*The Huffington Post*

About Wisdom Publications

Wisdom Publications is the leading publisher of classic and contemporary Buddhist books and practical works on mindfulness. To learn more about us or to explore our other books, please visit our website at wisdomexperience.org or contact us at the address below.

Wisdom Publications
199 Elm Street
Somerville, MA 02144 USA

We are a 501(c)(3) organization, and donations in support of our mission are tax deductible.

Wisdom Publications is affiliated with the Foundation for the Preservation of the Mahayana Tradition (FPMT).